D0397986

AMELIA
EARHART

THE AMERICAN HEROES SERIES

Amelia Earhart: The Sky's No Limit by Lori Van Pelt
Chief Joseph: Guardian of the People by Candy Moulton

FORTHCOMING

John Muir: Magnificent Tramp by Rod Miller
Mary Edwards Walker: Above and Beyond by Dale L. Walker
David Crockett: Hero of the Common Man by William Groneman III
George Washington: First in War, First in Peace by James A. Crutchfield

Dale L. Walker, General Editor

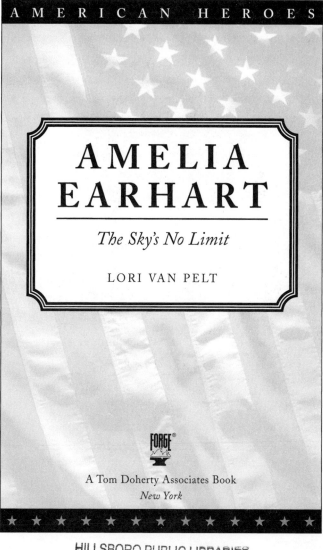

AMERICAN HEROES

AMELIA EARHART

The Sky's No Limit

LORI VAN PELT

FORGE

A Tom Doherty Associates Book
New York

Book design by Michael Collica

A Forge Book
Published by Tom Doherty Associates, LLC
175 Fifth Avenue, New York, NY 10010

www.tor.com

Forge® is a registered trademark of
Tom Doherty Associates, LLC.

Library of Congress Cataloging-in-Publication Data

Van Pelt, Lori, 1961–
    Amelia Earhart : the sky's no limit / Lori Van Pelt. — 1st ed.
      p. cm. — (American heroes series)
    "A Tom Doherty Associates book."
    Includes bibliographical references (p. 224) and index (p. 229).
    ISBN 0-765-31061-9 *3207 9708 865*
    EAN 978-0765-31061-3
    1. Earhart, Amelia, 1897–1937. 2. Air pilots—United States—
Biography. 3. Women air pilots—United States—Biography. I. Title.

TL540.E3V36 2005
629.13'092—dc22
[B]
                                                          2004056316

First Edition: March 2005

PRINTED IN THE UNITED STATES OF AMERICA

0 9 8 7 6 5 4 3 2 1

Contents

Contents

Foreword

The American newspaper reader of 1937 paused at the news that Japan had invaded China, that somebody named Neville Chamberlain had become prime minister of Britain, that the Duke of Windsor had married an American divorcée named Wallis Simpson, and that the Golden Gate Bridge had opened in San Francisco. The reader frowned at items about labor disputes and sit-down strikes, skimmed the columns of type on Rockefeller Center and the Lincoln Tunnel opening in New York, and in others learned that the average new house cost a bit over $4,000, a new car averaged $760, that gasoline had jumped to twenty-five cents a gallon, and coffee was becoming a luxury at thirty-eight cents a pound.

Two events of 1937 captured every reader's full attention, both, oddly, aviation stories, and both tragedies.

On May 6 the German dirigible *Hindenburg* exploded

while mooring at the Naval Air Station at Lakehurst, New Jersey, killing thirty-six people.

On July 2 Amelia Earhart, flying around the world in a twin-engine Lockheed Electra, and her navigator Fred Noonan disappeared somewhere in the South Pacific.

The *Hindenburg* calamity was caught on film and narrated by an anguished reporter on radio, but its victims were unknown to the average newspaper reader.

The Amelia Earhart news was different, personal; everybody knew Amelia.

To see those grainy films of her climbing into the cockpit of her airplane or chatting with fans, reporters, and friends is to be drawn to her. Willowy, pretty, charming, this tomboy Kansan, with her gap-toothed smile and infectious laugh, was irresistible. The proverbial crowned heads of Europe loved her. Presidents Coolidge, Hoover, and Franklin Roosevelt were among her admirers (and First Lady Eleanor Roosevelt took an airplane ride with her), as were Charles Lindbergh, Richard Byrd, Bernt Balchen, Ruth Nichols, and other aviation pioneers. The National Geographic Society honored her with its Gold Medal, the Army Air Force with its Distinguished Flying Cross.

For all the international renown and adulation, to her public Amelia seemed an innocent, content to fly airplanes, set records, smile and wave in ticker-tape parades, while her career was steered, often shrewdly, at times crassly, by her publisher husband, George Palmer Putnam. But while genuinely shy and self-effacing, Amelia was anything but a corn-fed rustic. She drove automobiles and flew airplanes in an era when a woman's place was still widely believed to be in the home, ignored such conventions, and championed, through her lectures and writings, the efforts of women to explore careers traditionally held by men. She urged women to "try to do things as men have tried" and to treat failure as a challenge to those who followed.

She knew her worth as an individual, too, and did not relish the incessant "Lady Lindy" comparisons in the press to her celebrated contemporary Charles A. Lindbergh. She enjoyed the opportunities that opened to her in 1928 after her journey in the Fokker trimotor *Friendship* across the Atlantic, a happenstance that gave her the honor of being the first woman to cross the ocean in an airplane, but she apologized to Anne Morrow, Lindbergh's wife, for the "Lady Lindy" business and was careful to point out to others that she was merely a *passenger* on the flight. Not until four years later, when she flew solo across the ocean in her Lockheed Vega, was she somewhat mollified in being compared to Lindbergh. Still, she sought more, not just women's records but *records*: altitude, speed, cross-country, Hawaii to San Francisco, Mexico City to New York, the "world at its waistline."

In her private life as well, Amelia knew what she wanted and was not timid in getting it. After Putnam wore her down, she agreed to marry him only when he agreed to certain conditions: She would pursue her flying career without interruption, needed time alone, and would not be housebound or bound, period. Her pioneering prenuptial agreement letter to Putnam even stated that if the marriage didn't work out, they would part amicably.

In this biography, author Lori Van Pelt sought out such aspects of Amelia Earhart's character to probe beneath the conventional "intrepid aviator" celebrity and presents an admiring ("What's not to admire?" the author says) but level story. There is the daring, driven, record-seeking Amelia, serving as pitchwoman for Hawaiian sugar, cigarettes (she did not smoke), a line of clothing, and whatever else was necessary to finance her single, expensive passion in life—flying. There is the scared and sometimes inept Amelia, stalling, ground-looping, and otherwise crashing airplanes and thinking of death. There is the secretive, stern, and demanding Amelia, trying to keep her alcoholic father, and her distressed mother and sister, together and out of debt. And, there is the publicly accessible Amelia—a lovable, laughing, seemingly carefree woman viewing the world by flying over it.

Van Pelt says, "I admire her perseverance, from that moment in 1920 when she made her first flight until 1937 when she made the last one. And, I love her independence of spirit, her zest for living, and her determination to do what she most wanted to do in life despite social traditions and the attitudes of family and friends that could have limited her."

In 1937 Amelia Earhart decided to fly around the world "at its waistline"—the equator. "Here was shining adventure, beckoning with new experiences," she said.

All forty years of her life Amelia Earhart epitomized that phrase, "shining adventure." It described her heart's desire from the moment in her youth when she first saw an airplane; from the time during World War I when she worked in a Toronto military hospital and heard tales of derring-do from wounded airmen returned from the Western Front; and especially after she earned her pilot's wings while yet in her twenties. Even after, she sought shining adventure beyond fame or even happiness, and she embodies the idea to this day, sixty-seven years since she vanished somewhere in the Pacific Ocean.

DALE L. WALKER

AMELIA EARHART

Prologue

The endless black ocean deepened the bleak loneliness Amelia Earhart felt that May night in 1932. The roar of the bright red Lockheed Vega's single engine, on takeoff deafening and in flight a mesmerizing drone, was her only companion as she directed the plane eastward twelve thousand feet above the Atlantic. This plane, her second of the Lockheed design, had been thoroughly reconditioned and refitted with a larger Pratt and Whitney Wasp engine, and she felt comfortable piloting the ship—it was the same craft she'd flown three years earlier in the first Women's Air Derby. Nor was the ocean a new experience. She had flown with two male pilots in the trimotor Fokker *Friendship* in 1928, earning global recognition for merely tagging along. Now, sailing above the black immensity, she flew across the Atlantic alone.

Four hours into her journey, the altimeter, measuring altitude, dipped and spun; the plane descended rapidly. The instrument had not failed her in twelve years of flying, but she knew from her training she could concentrate on the airspeed needle and focus on the horizon indicator to stay aloft. The barograph, a separate sealed device installed to measure altitude, could tell her only of the changes in height she made, but it might prove helpful.

About the same time that the altimeter malfunctioned, lightning flashed through the dark clouds, gusting winds buffeted the Vega, and rain whipped against the windshield. She increased the throttle and pulled back the stick in hopes of climbing above the tempest, aimed for what she hoped was twelve thousand feet but had no way of knowing the altitude with certainty. Strong downdrafts within the storm pushed against the Vega's upward motion. The moon shone briefly through a break in the thick clouds. She glanced at the instrument panel. The Sperry directional gyrocompass, a new addition for this flight, provided what she hoped would be trustworthy guidance. She relied on the gyro to keep her on course for the remainder of the flight.

Slush collected on the windshield, and the plane's response to her actions with stick and rudder grew sluggish. As she worked, she thought of the blooming dogwood beneath her bedroom window at her Rye, New York, home bidding her a "radiant farewell" when she departed.

Suddenly one wing pitched high, causing the ice-laden plane to spin wildly and begin a frighteningly rapid descent. Precious seconds sped past as the dark sea raced toward her. She struggled to regain control, pushed the stick forward, watched her airspeed increase, then pressed the rudder pedal opposite the wing with her foot and managed to bring the Vega's nose level, chanced a glance out the triangular cockpit window and saw whitecaps breaking beneath her. The barograph indicated a precipitous three-thousand-foot dip. She flew perilously close to the sea but kept the plane on that course, expecting the lower altitude would help melt the ice. When the airplane's wings sliced through layers of fog and clouds drifting near the ocean, she climbed again hoping to discover a safe altitude between the icy heights and the stormy ocean. She leveled off, took a deep breath. Her heart pounded from the close call, but hours spent in practice flying preparing for this journey kept her calm.

As she ascended, the controls again grew sluggish and slush again collected on the windshield. She was uncertain of her exact altitude and aimed the plane again toward the sea. Clouds and fog. She flew lower, again seeing whitecaps. Too low, she would crash into the ocean; too high and wing ice would push the plane into the water. After a couple of experiments, she discovered a workable middle level and stayed the course, concentrated on the instrument panel, ignored the broken barograph, and relied on the gyrocompass.

Now bursts of flames streaming from the exhaust streaked the darkness. She peered out the cockpit window; steady flames licked the exhaust manifold. She thought briefly of returning to her takeoff field at Harbor Grace, Newfoundland, but turning back offered no safer option than flying ahead. The Vega remained fuel heavy even after several hours of flight, and with the added hazard of the fire, attempting to land on the unlighted field at Harbor Grace was far too dangerous.

Like Charles Lindbergh, the first person to solo the Atlantic, exactly five years to the day earlier, Amelia had practiced flying "blind," relying only upon her instruments, and like "Lucky Lindy" she had her plane fitted to accommodate extra gasoline—420 gallons total. Lindbergh had bet his life on the extra gas rather than taking along a navigator, figuring that he would need the extra fuel if he missed his mark and was forced to fly along the French coast before heading to Paris. His 3,160-mile flight to his landing at Le Bourget field proved his point. Amelia's plane, with its additional gasoline, had a flying range of approximately thirty-two hundred miles.

The fire spurting from the exhaust manifold unsettled her. The stinging odor of gasoline fumes, always strong in the closed cockpit and even more so with the larger fuel tanks located right behind her, irritated her eyes and made her stomach queasy. Blinking back the involuntary tears, she spotted a steady drip from the reserve fuel tank, the leak that likely caused and fed the flames in the exhaust. Her options were few: She could ditch and, if she was lucky enough to survive impact and not drown, hope for rescue. She could gamble on reaching the coastline of France before burnout. She flew on.

Fourteen hours and fifty-six minutes after departing Newfoundland, she landed in Culmore, near London-derry, Ireland, the first woman to solo the Atlantic.

Tomboy

In 1903 two brothers, bicycle-makers from Dayton, Ohio, dared to believe that their new invention, a flying machine built of spruce and ash, its wings encased with muslin, and powered by their unique four-cylinder engine, could sail above the ground. To test their theory, they attempted flight on December 17 at Kitty Hawk, North Carolina. For four years the Wrights had been perfecting their designs and inventions, working toward this moment.

Younger brother Orville lay prone near the engine, centered in the forty-foot wingspan, his left hand at the ready to operate the elevator controls. Wilbur ran alongside as the craft sped along a launching rail, heading into the twenty-seven mile per hour wind. He stopped, watching as the Flyer lifted from the ground and carried his brother aloft.

Orville felt the wind slap his cheeks and smelled the salty scent of the sea as he flew. Shifting his hips from side to side helped move the wings and controlled the rudder. Twelve seconds later, barely enough time to realize he'd sailed across the sand, he landed 120 feet from his takeoff point. Exuberant with his success, he turned the airplane over to Wilbur for his chance to take flight. The brothers each flew twice more, and Wilbur controlled the craft for the final flight, remaining airborne for almost a full minute and traveling 852 feet.

A swift gust of wind struck the little girl's cheeks, blowing her long hair behind her and skewing the huge bow secured to her light brown locks. She wrinkled her nose at the force buffeting her and tightened her grip on the sides of the wooden cart as it sped along the track greased with household lard. Suddenly the cart jumped the rails and carried her into the air. At nearly the same time, the wind stopped and she felt a corresponding drop in her tummy. Almost before she realized she was falling, the cart crashed into the ground. She heard her sister scream as she bounced forward and bumped her lip hard against the wood just before it cracked and splintered. Shaking from the impact and thrilled by the adventure, seven-year-old Amelia Earhart climbed from the wreckage and gazed at the top of the toolshed, eight feet high, where she had begun her journey to the lawn. Her lip stung but the stunt had been *fun*.

Adults came running at the scream and crashing noise in the backyard of the Otis home in Atchison, Kansas. Grandmother Amelia Harres Otis scolded her charge, perturbed not only at her namesake grandchild and younger sister, Muriel, but at her own brother, Carl, for having assisted the girls and a neighbor boy in such a dangerous, foolish, and unladylike venture as building what they called a "roller coaster." Mrs. Otis adhered to the standards of the time and expected her granddaughters to behave properly and conform to the social mores of 1904 by wearing dresses and hair bows and playing with dolls. The incident she'd just witnessed definitely did not square with her view of ladylike behavior.

Amelia's roller-coaster idea sprang from her fascination with an amusement park ride she'd seen when her father took his family to the St. Louis World's Fair that year. Despite her attempt at creating a backyard version of the amusement ride and the exuberant feeling of flight she enjoyed while riding it, her passion for airplanes was not ignited during her childhood, but came later in her life. Still, as a child she continued to try anything, to test the limits of her physical abilities by doing things the little boys of her age and day enjoyed, like sledding down hills headfirst and exploring forbidden caves.

In Atchison, Mrs. Otis persevered in her efforts to mold her rambunctious tomboy into a proper young lady. Amelia and Muriel, three years her junior, stayed with their mother's parents for many years while their father worked as a much-traveled lawyer, settling claims for the railroad; his wife, Amy, often accompanied him on his business trips.

The young daughters of Amy Otis and Edwin Stanton Earhart enjoyed many happy times in the home of their maternal grandparents, unaware of Judge Alfred Otis's displeasure with his daughter's choice of husband. He had hoped Amy would marry a man with better prospects. His ancestors included James Otis, whose protest against certain British laws was thought to have contributed to the American Revolution. He had himself worked first as an attorney, eventually serving as a district court judge, and after retiring in 1908, he became the president of the Atchison Savings Bank. Along the way he made astute land speculation deals and accumulated a modest fortune.

At age sixteen, Amy Otis suffered a hearing loss from typhoid fever but did not allow the setback to hinder her life. A child of culture and opportunity, she was raised in her parents' nine-room home on Quality Hill overlooking the Missouri River, and was accustomed to having the accouterments of wealth—pleasant surroundings, with books, piano, and riding stables, her routine daily needs tended to by servants. She enjoyed riding horses and loved to dance. The judge often took her with him when he evaluated land used for security against loans or for investment purposes. Sometimes he traveled at the request of the Trinity Episcopal Church, where he served as senior warden, scouting out ministerial candidates.

Amy had been accepted to Vassar in 1889, but a severe

bout of diphtheria prevented her from enrolling. She decided against continuing her education, choosing instead to accompany her father on trips to the Far West. On one such excursion to Colorado in 1890, the group he was meeting with invited him and Amy to join them in climbing Pike's Peak. They traveled halfway up by horseback, camped and rested for part of the night, and started out again soon after midnight to make the final four-hour climb in time to see the sunrise from the top of the mountain. Amy was the only female in the group to tackle the final ascent and, upon arriving at the crest, discovered she was the first woman to make the entire climb.

That same year she fell in love. Edwin Earhart, a young law student and friend of the Otis's son, Mark, captured her heart at her coming-out party. He did not measure up to Judge Otis's expectations. The judge had decreed that any young man hoping for Amy's hand in marriage would have to make at least $50 per month in income in order to support her properly. To meet the condition and win the hand of the woman he loved, Edwin worked for five years before he earned as much from his law practice. The judge reluctantly allowed the marriage, presenting the young couple with a furnished house in Kansas City, Kansas, as a wedding gift.

Edwin worked settling claims for the Rock Island and other railroads. His work frequently took him away, and Amy grew lonely for her parents, brothers, sisters, and cousins, and visited her family often. The couple's first child was stillborn. During Amy's second pregnancy she stayed with her parents, and Amelia Mary Earhart, the namesake of her two grandmothers, was born on July 24, 1897, in the Otis home on Quality Hill in Atchison.

Even after Judge Otis realized the depth of Amy's devotion to her husband and after she provided him with grandchildren, he did not soften much toward his son-in-law. Edwin, always well intentioned, had little financial sense. One example of this, recounted by Muriel Earhart Morrissey in her book, *Courage Is the Price,* involved the family's trip to the St. Louis World's Fair. Edwin had earned $100 in some railroad claim cases and promptly spent the entire amount on the family outing. This impulsive expenditure came on the heels of a fuss with bill collectors seeking tax money. Amy had saved money from her household allowance and gave the funds to her husband, expecting him to pay the taxes with the cash, but instead of abiding by her instructions, Edwin attempted to secure a patent on a railroad signal flag holder he had invented. In filing for the patent, he discovered the invention had already been created and patented.

Amy, who had never worried about money, had to learn to live frugally, and her parents blamed Edwin for being an inadequate provider. The resulting tension eventually drove him to liquor, further worsening his marital and financial problems.

Edwin Earhart came from a large family, much poorer than the Otis clan. His father, Reverend David Earhart, was an Evangelical Lutheran missionary with twelve children and hoped that Edwin would follow in his footsteps and take up theological studies. Edwin, however, wanted to study law and graduated from Thiel College in Pennsylvania and then the University of Kansas law school after shining shoes, tutoring other students, and performing whatever work he could find to pay the tuition and buy the books.

Amy loved him and, after they were married, traveled with him. Their children stayed with them in Kansas City in the summers and spent winters in Atchison with their grandparents. As a result, Amelia and Muriel experienced both financial ease and tension as youngsters.

Edwin, when at home on visits, showered his daughters with fatherly affection and played games with them. The two girls especially enjoyed one game they called "Bogie," climbing into an old carriage stored in the Otis's barn and from the seats of the dusty wagon imagining traveling to a variety of faraway places. The game awakened the wanderlust in Amelia, although such daydreaming was not considered "ladylike" in the early 1900s when a woman's place was in the home caring for a husband rather than traipsing off to distant lands, or even dreaming of such traipsing.

While she later wrote wistfully, "Unfortunately, I lived at a time when girls were still girls," she played basketball and tennis, rode bicycles and horses, and slept with a wooden donkey rather than a doll. Her father gave Amelia a .22-caliber rifle for Christmas the year she turned nine, and she used it to shoot rats in the barn, persuading her horrified grandmother that she was helping to prevent anybody from catching the plague. Amy Otis Earhart once sent bloomer-style gym suits to her girls, and the gift sent Grandmother Otis into a tizzy about proper attire for young ladies. The girls were delighted; Amelia recalled feeling "terribly free and athletic." When wearing the attire advocated by suffragette Amelia Jenks Bloomer, she admitted, "We also felt somewhat as outcasts among the little girls who fluttered about us in their skirts."

Photographs of the time show the Earhart girls bowing to convention by wearing their long hair in braids with huge bows as befitted young women of their era. Amelia later wrote, "Tradition hampers just as much as clothing."

A sled was another Christmas gift their grandmother felt would have been better suited to boys. Amelia loved "belly-slamming," riding the sled with her chest pressed against the wood and her head stuck out front. On one occasion, she zoomed down an icy hill and nearly collided head-on with the junk man and his horse and carriage. The horse wore blinders and didn't see the child careening toward him, and the deliveryman apparently did not hear the ruckus raised by the children at the top of the hill who could see the accident waiting to happen. Luckily, Amelia slid between the horse's legs with no harm done to animal, man, or carriage.

In addition to their tomboy pursuits, the girls enjoyed the quieter pastime of books, taking turns reading aloud to each other while tending housekeeping chores. In their grandparents' library, they read *The Youth's Companion,*

Harper's Young People, Harper's Weekly, Puck, Oliver Optic's Success Stories for Boys, along with the works of Charles Dickens, Victor Hugo, and Alexandre Dumas. Amelia excelled in her studies at the College Preparatory School the girls attended in Atchison. Sarah Walton, a teacher, wrote of her: "The joy of achievement was uppermost in Amelia's mind. The prizes at school as the plaudits and awards of the world were secondary to her personal satisfaction in a job well done."

When she reached seventh grade and Muriel the fourth, their father became head of the railroad claims department with his salary almost doubled. The promotion required moving to Des Moines, Iowa, in 1907, with his family joining him there the next year. While in Des Moines in 1908, Amelia saw her first airplane at the Iowa State Fair, but at the time she found the fifteen-cent peach basket hat she wanted to buy much more appealing than the wood and wire vehicle displayed on the grounds.

During their first year in Iowa her mother chose to have her daughters privately tutored, but although Edwin was prospering, the $25 per month tutoring fee proved too expensive, so Amy asked the girls' teachers for assignments in advance so that they could keep up with their studies even while taking trips with their father. In the summertime the sisters stayed near Lake Okabena in Minnesota, where they rode horses, played tennis, fished, and even milked cows. Evenings were spent listening to popular music of the day—on the Victrola.

By 1910 Edwin Earhart's alcoholism had become a

pernicious part of the family's life. That year he was fired from his job, tried to "take the cure," but failed. Muriel recalled that once when Amelia helped him pack for a business trip, she discovered a whiskey bottle hidden in one of his socks. She poured it down the sink, and when Edwin, drunk, threatened to strike his beloved daughter, Amy had to intervene. That day, thirteen-year-old Amelia learned a rough lesson, understanding that even her father's love for her could not overcome his addiction. She was emotionally hurt by his alcoholism and grew protective of her mother and sister—in later years, domineering.

In 1910 Mrs. Otis suffered a lengthy illness and died. Amy had gone to stay with her mother to help nurse her through her final days while the girls stayed with their father. Amelia, her grandmother's favorite, felt bereft but kept her emotions concealed, a familiar trait throughout her life.

Mrs. Otis left an estate worth an estimated million dollars. In her will, she split the sum among her surviving children but placed a special restriction upon the funds designated for Amy, requiring that the money be placed in trust for twenty years or until Edwin's death. The move was intended to protect Amy and the girls from Edwin's fiscal fallibility. When he lost his job, the family survived on the meager earnings from the trust fund.

In the spring of 1913 the Earharts moved to St. Paul, Minnesota, where Edwin had found work as a freight clerk for the Great Northern Railway. But again his drinking cost him the job.

With an opportunity for a position with the Chicago, Burlington, & Quincy Railroad in Springfield, Missouri, he took his family there only to discover the employee he was to replace had changed his mind. At this point, Amy took action to protect her family until Edwin could find stable work. She and the girls traveled to Chicago and moved in with some former Kansas City friends who had offered to help.

Amelia had attended six high schools in four years, but finally settled at Hyde Park High School where she enjoyed science classes, especially chemistry and physics, as well as math, but kept to herself. The caption beneath her yearbook photograph read, "The girl in brown who walks alone." She graduated in 1916, and afterward the family moved to Kansas City once again to live with Edwin, now working as an independent lawyer—and a sober one.

Soon after the family was reunited, he persuaded Amy to break her mother's will and use the money rather than having it locked away. Although Amy felt uneasy pursuing litigation against her own relatives, they took the case to court. The judge, after hearing from Mrs. Otis's doctor, who declared her to have been incompetent due to excess worry and ill health at the time she made her last testament, decided in Amy's favor and dissolved the trust. Her brother Mark had been in charge of investing the funds and had made some poor management choices that significantly depleted the principal. Amy received $60,000. This was a substantial amount in 1916 but much less than Mrs. Otis had intended when she had arranged the trust. Still, the money permitted Amy to send Amelia to the all-girls Ogontz School in Rydal, Pennsylvania, north of Philadelphia, that fall. She had hoped Vassar would admit Amelia, but her application reached the college too late for consideration.

Of Amelia at this period in her life, Jean Backus, in her book, *Letters from Amelia*, wrote that she "was nineteen, slim and intense, more often frowning than smiling, a fine scholar, and an introvert subject to conflicting emotions generated by her stubborn opposition to certain conventions of society and habits of the family." The Ogontz headmistress, Abbie Sutherland-Brown, wrote, "Amelia was always pushing into unknown seas in her thinking, her reading, and in experiments in science. Her most vivid characteristic was her intellectual curiosity which burned brightly when she was with us and was certainly exemplified by her later career."

Amelia wrote often to her mother in the fall of 1916, mentioning her attendance at a Philadelphia Symphony concert with five others and outlining her schedule. The students were awakened at 7:00 A.M. by cowbell, followed by prayers and sit-ups, breakfast, and a morning walk. Her classes began at nine and ended at two in the afternoon, following which, she played hockey, basketball, or tennis. A late-afternoon study hall preceded dinner, a dress-up occasion. Her classes included French and German, spelling, current events, Bible instruction, and art.

The following summer, she vacationed with her father at Saugatuck, on Lake Michigan, and that fall was elected the vice president of her class and secretary of the Red Cross chapter the school organized to help with the war effort following the entrance of the United States into the European conflict. Her courses included modern drama, literature, German and German literature, French, arithmetic, and logic.

During her eighteen-month stay at Ogontz, she began compiling a scrapbook of newspaper clippings detailing the historical and contemporary achievements of women: authors, film producers, fire lookouts, play directors, physicians, explorers, travelers, a pistol champion, lecturers, a city manager, singers, psychologists, the only female game warden, upholsterers, farmers, a police commissioner, and eventually a clipping on the United States assistant attorney general Mable Walker Willebrandt.

Amelia paid a visit to Muriel, then living in Toronto and attending St. Margaret's College, for Christmas 1917. Their mother had gone to live there that fall, taking residence in an apartment hotel. Along with others from the Ogontz school, Amelia had been knitting items for the troops in France. After the holiday, in February 1918, she returned to Toronto, determined to become a nurse. The sight of four men recently returned from the Western Front walking down King Street had a profound effect on her. The men, each of whom had lost a leg in battle, hobbled along on their crutches supporting one another. She decided to leave Ogontz without graduating to concentrate on taking an active role in the war effort.

Aloft

I n Toronto, Amelia immersed herself in caring for
wounded men returned from the war. She took
a Voluntary Aid Detachment course and a Red
Cross first-aid class, then began working at Spadina
Military Hospital in Toronto in the spring of 1918,
thinking about studying medicine. Twelve-hour shifts
at the hospital provided some practical experience toward that end, but she also scrubbed floors, washed
dishes, carried food trays to patients, and helped in the
dietary department. Through her hospital work, she met
many injured combat pilots and developed a camaraderie with them, listening to their conversations when
they went "ground flying"—talking about their adventures in the air. Muriel wrote, "Their modesty and reti-
cence about their exploits and their fatalistic attitude
toward life appealed to Amelia."

Amelia later wrote of attending a flying exposition in Toronto around the time of the Armistice and watching a war ace perform stunts. After twenty minutes in the air, the pilot began to dive toward the crowd gathered on the field. Amelia watched a couple of times, then stood directly beneath the plane, aware of the danger, and gazed up at the machine as it flew past. She wrote, "I did not understand it at the time but I believe that little red airplane said something to me as it swished by."

She stayed in Toronto until November 1918. The Armistice that month marked a period of ill health for Amelia. She had worked stressful night duty shifts on a pneumonia ward and escaped the influenza pandemic that year but contracted a sinus infection that would plague her throughout her life. She was hospitalized and would later undergo periodic irrigation treatments and surgeries for sinusitis.

While recuperating, she stayed with her mother and sister in Northampton, Massachusetts. Amy had moved there in the spring of 1919 to live with Muriel, then attending the Capen School to take some additional classes. In Northampton, Amelia bought a banjo from a pawnshop. She had been a member of the Mandolin Club at Ogontz and transferred her mandolin skills to the banjo. As she regained her strength, Amelia found another outlet for her energies: She studied automotive mechanics.

That fall, she entered Columbia University as a premedical student and took two chemistry classes and others in organic and inorganic biology. She enjoyed her classes but decided against working directly with patients and changed her mind about becoming a physician, focusing instead on medical research.

In 1920 she traveled to Los Angeles to stay with her parents as they tried to reconcile. Edwin had moved there to continue his work settling railroad claims. Amelia felt restless and uncertain as to what career she should choose. She left Columbia in May, and soon after, at her parents' home in California, met one of the Earharts' boarders, Sam Chapman, a New England engineer, and began dating him.

Her fascination with flying had not dimmed since she left Toronto. She attended air meets every weekend, and Edwin took her to the Winter Air Tournament on Christmas Day, 1920, at the official opening of a new airfield in Long Beach, where they saw air races, aerobatics, and wing-walking exhibitions. She was thrilled with the experience and decided to take flying lessons. She had her father inquire into this possibility, and three days later, Edwin, although uneasy about the whole idea, accompanied her to Rogers Field and bought her a ticket for an airplane ride.

Barnstormer Frank Hawks, a pilot who later became celebrated for his speed records, took Amelia on her first flight, a "joy-hop," as Amelia described the short circuit around the flying field, and as they gained a few hundred feet of altitude, her anxieties drifted away. "As soon as we left the ground, I knew I myself had to fly," she later wrote.

Lessons cost one dollar per minute, and a total of $1,000 to prepare a pilot to receive a license. The Earharts did not have the money, but Amelia arranged for Kinner Field pilot Neta Snook to train her, to be paid with Liberty Bonds once Amelia began work with a local telephone company. She chose a woman pilot as a teacher intentionally, believing she would feel less intimidated and more relaxed than with a male instructor.

Snook had learned to fly in 1917, becoming the first female graduate of the Curtiss School of Aviation, operated by Glenn Hammond Curtiss. He was originally a motorcycle designer and racer who also experimented with airplanes and had been involved in patent wars with the Wright Brothers in the early 1900s.

(Although unable to break the Wright patents, Curtiss worked with the financial backing of Alexander Graham Bell through the Aerial Experiment Association and built the first United States Army dirigible in 1905. In 1910 Curtiss won $10,000 from the *New York World* for flying from Albany to New York, a distance of 152 miles, in two hours and forty-six minutes. He also sponsored teams of racing and exhibition pilots who competed for hefty monetary prizes.)

Neta Snook, just a year older than Amelia, owned a Canuck, the Canadian version of the Curtiss Jenny used as a wartime trainer. The two-seater biplane, equipped with a ninety horsepower 0X-5 engine, contained dual controls, allowing the student to sit in front and the instructor to monitor performance from the backseat.

Snook often carried along a rubber mallet to tap the trainee on the head in case the new pilot froze from fright at the controls. By shouting directions and kicking the panel between the seats to indicate when to stop or go, the teacher communicated with her pupil.

When Snook first met the Earharts, Amelia wore a brown suit and had wound her long braids around her head. The veteran pilot "liked her on sight," and wrote in her book, *I Taught Amelia to Fly*, "She would have stood out in any crowd."

Snook recalled that Amelia's first training flight on January 3, 1921, lasted thirty minutes and consisted mostly of taxiing up and down the field so she could get the feel of the rudder. The next day, Amelia brought along a library book on aerodynamics and wore her "breeks," the clothes she'd worn while riding horseback and also found suitable for airplane piloting. Snook recalled, "They were dark brown pants, tight fitting from the knee down. The inside of each leg contained a patch of reinforced leather as a preventive from saddle chafing. Laced boots reached to midcalf. She wore a neat, tight-fitting jacket to match. It was a beautifully tailored outfit."

During the first two months of training, Amelia logged only four hours of airtime because of foggy or windy weather. She rode the streetcars to the end of the line, then walked three miles farther to arrive at Kinner Field, located near Huntington Park. Snook described Amelia as "a serious student," and "a loner" who helped out at her father's law office while continuing her work in the mail room at the telephone company and taking on additional part-time work in a local photographic studio.

Caught up in the romance of flying, she even adopted the dress of the veteran pilots, breeches, cap, goggles, and leather coat. When the men ribbed her about her new leather jacket, she slept in it and spotted it with oil stains so it appeared suitably wrinkled and broken in. She began to cut her long light brown hair, in stages and secretly, so as not to be suddenly noticeable, until she arrived at the tousled bob that eventually became her signature hairstyle.

While her clothing may have helped her look like a pilot, instructor Snook believed her student's skills came naturally. If the weather was good, they flew daily, and Snook kept a close eye on her student when the two took to the air. Two high-tension wire lines, just eight feet apart, ran alongside Long Beach Boulevard and had to be cleared before landing, but Snook said Amelia "would have gone between them if I didn't watch her all the time."

There is no official record of Amelia's first lone flight, but she was required to solo before passing the examination for a National Aeronautic Association license. She passed it on December 15, 1921, and in her book, *20 Hrs., 40 Mins.,* said one of her shock absorbers broke on her first attempt, forcing her to return to the field uncertain as to what she had done wrong. On the second try, she took the plane up to five thousand feet and "made a thoroughly rotten landing."

On her twenty-fifth birthday, July 24, 1922, Amelia bought Bert Kinner's creation, the Kinner Airster, for $2,000. Her mother helped with the money. The biplane had a seventeen-foot wingspan, and a three-cylinder, radial, air-cooled Lawrance 60-horsepower engine. A lighter, more unstable, and less powerful craft than the Canuck trainer, the Airster required piloting adjustments, including gentler banking and speedier landings. Snook described the plane as behaving "like a leaf in the air" and thought the machine too dangerous for beginners. Amelia recalled, "The motor was so rough that my feet went to sleep after more than a few minutes on the rudder bar." She painted her biplane yellow, referred to it as the "Kinner *Canary*," and allowed the plane to be used in sales demonstrations to pay hangar fees.

Crashes were inevitable. Snook recalled flying with Amelia about six miles from Kinner Field to Goodyear Field to see Donald W. Douglas's new Cloudster biplane, the first to carry its own weight in payload. They managed the short distance easily but on the return trip struck a stand of eucalyptus trees near the end of the Goodyear runway. The Airster, plagued by a clogged cylinder, couldn't climb fast enough for Amelia to avoid them. Her choices were to push the nose down to help the airplane gain speed or to pull up and stall. She stalled and smashed into the trees, damaging the propeller and landing gear. Snook, who said she would have made the same choice, disentangled from the wreckage, looked back to check on Amelia, and found her student pilot had bitten her tongue, but stood calmly powdering her nose. "'We have to look nice when the reporters come,' she reminded me," her instructor said.

Another mishap occurred when Amelia once neglected to check the airplane's fuel supply, resulting in an engine failure not long after takeoff. Her exasperated teacher took the controls, landed in a cabbage patch, and rebuked her student for the negligent behavior. Other times, she landed in mud, sticking the wheels tight, and in a field so thick with weeds that her plane came to a sudden halt, tipping over and ejecting her.

One day, Amelia told her flight trainer she wanted to learn to drive and had brought $20 with her so they could rent a car. Snook had a driver's license and drove the borrowed Model T Ford first, showing her protégée the controls. Amelia took the wheel on the return trip and fell in love with driving.

Scraping together funds to continue flight lessons, she paid for the instruction with Liberty Bonds and on credit. Her mother had helped her purchase her airplane, but Amy lost her money soon after through her investment in a gypsum mine venture. She had hoped to rebuild her financial foundation when her capital dwindled to $20,000, and she invested in the mine managed by Peter Barnes, a friend of Amelia's beau Sam Chapman. Amelia and her father also became involved, helping work at the mine near Las Vegas, Nevada, in early

1922 to speed production. One afternoon, a sudden rainstorm flooded a gully, washing out a bridge, and while Amelia, her father, and two of Barnes's friends made the crossing safely in a truck, Barnes followed in a second truck that overturned and trapped him in the water. All hope for monetary reward from the mine was lost. Amelia wrote to Muriel, "There is no way I can soften the blow for you. We have to take these things as they come. Peter is drowned, the mine irreparably flooded, and all of Mother's investment gone."

In the spring of 1922 Neta Snook married and gave up teaching. Her replacement, John "Monte" Montijo, was a former Army pilot who performed stunts for Goldwyn Studios, demonstrated the Airster, and owned a flying school across from Kinner Field. In August, Amelia began taking lessons from him. She wanted to learn aerobatics, and Montijo said she "handled the ship like a veteran and made a perfect takeoff and landing." While taking lessons from Snook, logging five hours of instruction in the Canuck and fifteen hours in the Airster, she had learned the basic skills to recover from spins and stalls. With Montijo, she performed more complicated exercises such as side slips to help with landings in tight spots, loops and rolls, lazy-eights and split-S's. As she advanced in her flight studies, he noticed her interest in the mechanics of the airplane as well.

On October 22, 1922, she participated in an air meet at Rogers Field not far from Kinner. She requested installation of a sealed barograph so that the Aero Club of Southern California, sponsor of the event, could record her altitude in the Airster. While her father and Muriel, who was now teaching in Huntington Beach, watched, she soared aloft twice, encountering fog and sleet but reaching fourteen thousand feet on her second attempt in the open-cockpit plane with no oxygen tank. A disconnected spark plug lever during the first try required her to land sooner than planned. During her second flight, the engine sputtered, and rather than let it stall, she forced a tailspin, pulling out when she descended below the fog at three thousand feet. Prior to the flight she said she had only planned "a calibration of the ceiling" for the Airster when in fact she wanted to set a women's altitude record. She achieved it but afterward was scolded by a veteran pilot who wanted to know what she would have done if the fog had settled at ground level.

On May 15, 1923, she received her pilot's license from the Fédération Aéronautique Internationale, the international aviation organization to which the American National Aeronautic Association belonged. Amelia was the sixteenth woman in the world who had earned the coveted paper.

Friendship

When the telephone call came one spring day in 1928, Amelia Earhart was working as a full-time staff social worker at Denison House, a settlement house in Boston. She was reluctant to tear herself away from her duties, which at that moment included rehearsing a play with her young Syrian and Chinese charges, but she heard a male voice asking if she'd like to try something new in aviation. The caller, Captain Hilton H. Railey, admitted the venture he proposed was dangerous, and he gave her excellent references. She checked them out, then had her supervisor, Marion Perkins, head worker at Denison House, accompany her that afternoon to Railey's office.

As soon as he saw her, he knew she was the right person for the project, even though he doubted her qualifications as a pilot. He had found the "Lady Lindy" sought by publisher George Palmer Putnam, who had been working with the sponsors of the enterprise, and who asked him to contact Amelia. He told her he was seeking the first woman to fly the Atlantic. She requested further details; he revealed what he could.

Would she do it?

"Yes," she said, and with that simple reply, she placed herself among those being considered for the *Friendship* flight, a journey that would change her life.

This transatlantic air crossing was the brainchild of Amy Guest of Philadelphia, who had married an Englishman, Frederick Guest, who had served in the Air Ministry of British Prime Minister David Lloyd George. Through the Atlantic flight, which would generate substantial publicity, she hoped to promote good relations between Britain and the United States. At first, she intended to be the first woman to cross the Atlantic Ocean in a heavier-than-air craft, but as the time for the risky venture neared, her family balked at her participation in the flight. Now she wanted another female, a typical American woman, to replace her and asked Putnam to find her.

Captain Railey, a newspaperman and friend of United States Navy Commander Richard Byrd, who had flown to the North Pole in 1926, said that Byrd's Fokker trimotor monoplane was to be used for the flight, and after hearing Amelia's excited "yes," Railey invited her to his office.

Earhart biographer John Burke wrote that Amelia impressed Railey as he learned of her competence and intelligence, and he said she looked like Charles Lindbergh, "with the same tousled blond hair, shyness, modesty, and all-American grin, and underlying them the same hard-rock sense of purpose."

Amelia's appearance and good manners likely cinched the deal even though her flight skills were still in development. She had logged five hundred flight hours but as yet had not developed instrument-only skills, nor had she any experience in a trimotor.

A ten-day waiting period followed the phone call. She had been instructed to arrange her affairs so that she could make the trip if called upon. Despite the success of Lindbergh in flying across the ocean on May 20, 1927, and the victorious journeys of four others since, fourteen people had died trying the same feat. In the days following Amelia's subsequent New York interview, Englishwoman Elsie Mackay and her escort, Captain Walter Hinchcliffe, disappeared over the Atlantic; American Ruth Elder, the fourth woman to try the crossing, landed in the ocean but survived her failed attempt with George Haldeman and was rescued three hundred miles from the Azores.

Because the *Friendship* flight was to remain secret until the actual event, she told only her supervisor about the flight. At the end of the waiting period, backers of the venture summoned Amelia to New York for an interview. In the office of New York publisher George Palmer Putnam she also faced Amy Guest's brother, John Phipps, and attorney David T. Layman, Jr. In writing of the interview, Amelia said she tried not to appear too anxious to be chosen lest the men "be loath to drown me," and yet she wanted to convey the impression that she would enjoy the trip. In truth, she was raring to go.

In 1924 a recurrence of her sinusitis had forced her to sell her Kinner *Canary,* and sadly, the man who bought the airplane crashed the Airster the first time he flew it and both he and his passenger were killed. Too ill to fly, she purchased a sleek, sporty automobile, a Kissel Kar, which she christened the *Yellow Peril,* and drove across the country with her mother, who had divorced Edwin that same year, riding along. They stopped at numerous national parks and racked up seven thousand miles before reaching Boston, where Muriel was now attending Harvard. Soon after their arrival, Amelia entered Massachusetts General Hospital for medical procedures to help ease her sinus problems and, while recuperating, spent a restless period. She attended Columbia University in New York that fall, then spent the summer of 1925 attending Harvard but never settling on a degree program. To help defray her expenses, she taught English courses.

Sam Chapman, who worked at Boston Edison Company, wanted to marry her, even offering to change jobs when he believed her hesitation resulted from a dislike of his work schedule. Although she liked Sam, she resisted. She did not want to become a housewife and told a friend she considered marriage "living the life of a domestic robot."

In the autumn of 1926 she accepted the position of social worker at Denison House in Boston and spent her spare time hanging around the airfield. She joined the Boston chapter of the National Aeronautic Association and became its vice president; worked with Harold T. Dennison, of Quincy, Massachusetts, a friend of Bert Kinner's, in establishing an airport at Squantum; and helped her old friend Kinner by hawking his airplane at every opportunity. When the Dennison Airport opened on July 2, 1927, a newspaper report listed her as a director and the only woman on the aviation staff. She continued taking flight instruction as well, paying $20 an hour to the Dennison Aviation Corporation and logging additional hours of airtime that autumn.

She enjoyed her social work with the children at Denison House, but Captain Railey's call thrilled her, and she soon learned of his group's decision. The others in charge of selecting the "Lady Lindy" who would join the transatlantic flight agreed with Railey that Amelia was the woman for the job. Upon hearing this, she discreetly arranged a leave of absence with her supervisor. She later told *The New York Times* it would have been "too inartistic to refuse" the offer to fly the Atlantic.

Amelia also confided in Sam Chapman, giving him her will and a letter for Muriel to be delivered after the plane took off. In the will, dated April 5, 1928, she listed debts of $1,000 for hospital and dental expenses and as assets her Kissel car, a United States bond, and stock in the Kinner Airplane Company and the Dennison Airport. She wanted her mother to receive the remaining funds after the debts had been paid. In her letter to Muriel, she explained, ". . . if I succeed, all will be well. If I don't I shall be happy to pop off in the middle of such an adventure." She prepared a separate letter for each of her parents and gave these to George Putnam. Those letters remained unopened for nine years.

During the interview in Putnam's office, she learned that the pilot, Wilmer Stultz, and the mechanic, Lou "Slim" Gordon, would receive $20,000 and $5,000 respectively for their contributions to the transatlantic flight. Amelia's only reward would be the opportunity to go along, earning recognition as the first woman to cross the Atlantic by air. Payment received on articles she wrote for newspapers, and royalties or advertising fees, would be donated to help finance the venture. She requested additional terms allowing her to check the equipment, to meet the pilot, and to fly at least part of the way. Following the interview, Amy Guest sent her the agreement for her participation in the ocean flight, designating her as "captain" and giving her authority to make certain decisions aboard the *Friendship*—power that the flight's backers, surprisingly, had made available to her. By naming a woman "captain," they probably hoped to help increase the publicity for the adventure— if she wished to accept the responsibility that accompanied the privileges of the title.

Even so, she dared not venture to the airfield to help with preparations because her presence might alert on-lookers that something unique was being planned. She saw the plane only twice before the trip. Stultz, also an expert radio operator, and the mechanic, Gordon, checked the plane at Boston Airport, took test flights, and attended to the necessary details there. Any curious observers would likely believe the plane was being outfitted for an upcoming flight by Commander Byrd. Together with Stultz and Gordon, and Commander Robert Elmer, who served as technical adviser, she met with Byrd at his home in Boston to discuss the transatlantic flight.

The plane, with its three 200-horsepower motors and huge seventy-two-foot wingspan, was equipped with pontoons and moored at East Boston's Jeffrey Yacht Club. Under normal conditions, the airplane carried just ninety-five gallons of fuel in two wing tanks. During the testing, additional fuel totaling one thousand pounds was added, carried mostly in the wing, but two additional fuel tanks were placed in the passenger cabin, where Amelia would sit for much of the journey. To help ease the plane's ascent on takeoff, the fuel load was decreased to seven hundred pounds. Small five-gallon cans of gasoline were also carried inside the aircraft, to be used to shift weight for better balance when necessary.

After New York meteorologist Dr. James "Doc" Kimball declared the ocean weather satisfactory for the flight, and when conditions in Boston became favorable, the crew, including backup pilot Lou Gower, rode the tugboat

Sadie Rose out to the yacht club and to the airplane. Amelia, awakened at three-thirty that morning, wore a white silk blouse and red scarf with her brown breeks, high-laced boots, leather jacket, cap, and goggles. She brought along another brown and white scarf and a beige sweater, as well as a fur-lined flying suit she borrowed from Major Charles H. Woolley, an Air National Guard pilot, to keep her warm when the cabin turned cold at higher altitudes. She carried a small flight logbook, a pair of binoculars, and a camera. Her personal items consisted of a toothbrush and comb, a few clean handkerchiefs, and a small tube of cold cream. For food, they carried a large thermos of coffee for the men and a smaller container filled with hot chocolate for herself, plus oranges and several sandwiches.

Gower planned to ride to Trepassey, Newfoundland, but during takeoff, prop winds caused the pontoons to create a strong suction, holding the heavy aircraft on the water. After another try, they discarded six of the five-gallon gasoline cans on board and Gower left the aircraft and rode to shore in a small boat.

On the third try, they taxied through the harbor, aided by a welcome breeze, and chugged aloft at about 6:30 A.M. on Sunday morning, June 3, 1928. A broken latch on the cabin door hampered them, but Amelia held the door shut until Gordon could leave his post and secure it by tying a rope anchored to a heavy gasoline can to the handle. The wind pushed the door open as they ascended, and when Amelia jumped on top of the gas can to prevent it from being dragged out of the plane, she nearly toppled outside. Gordon responded to her shouts by pulling her back into a more secure position and grabbing for the door. At about the same time, Stultz banked the plane, and the action pushed Gordon back and slammed the door shut. He secured the door this time with a leather strap.

Traveling at an average speed of 114 miles per hour and at an altitude of two thousand feet, they encountered thick fog beyond Halifax, Nova Scotia, then circled until Stultz saw the Naval Air Station through a break in the clouds and landed in Halifax Harbor after 9:00 A.M. He moored the plane in the harbor and went ashore with Gordon to check weather reports while Amelia waited in the trimotor and ate a ham sandwich. The men returned after the fog had dissipated and the crew took off but encountered poor conditions again and returned to Halifax.

The preflight secrecy disappeared in the plane's wake as it left Boston. George Putnam called a news conference following takeoff, and Railey disclosed the information that a female flier was bound for England. In Halifax, Stultz and Gordon went to a restaurant for dinner while Amelia, unaware of Putnam's publicity release, remained at their Dartmouth hotel. She later wrote of the inconsiderate journalists who sought photographs of Stultz and Gordon late into the night, disrupting their rest, snapped pictures before breakfast, and interviewed them during the meal and afterward.

After replacing about a hundred gallons of fuel, they took off at about 9:00 A.M. and reached Trepassey five hours later. Because word of the woman aboard had spread throughout the world by this time, numerous people boarded boats to greet the plane in the harbor, so many that Amelia said their "arrival resembled a rodeo." She found a convent near the airfield and visited with the nuns in an effort to escape the press while Stultz and Gordon fueled the plane.

The flight was stalled in Trepassey nearly two weeks due to bad weather over the Atlantic. George Putnam's frequent communications with the United States Weather Bureau in New York, telegraphed to Amelia, at least kept the flight crew updated. The reports, based on information received from ships at sea, took many hours to reach Trepassey.

In an article written for *The New York Times* after the flight, Amelia said the thirteen-day wait at Trepassey was the most difficult part of the flight. In her books, she recalled the kindness of the residents of the fishing town, but in *Last Flight* admitted she grew tired of endless meals of rabbit and mutton. From Newfoundland she wired her mother, telling her not to worry. Whatever the outcome, the gamble had been worthwhile, she said.

Amy Earhart, who had learned of the flight from a reporter before Sam Chapman could tell her, commented that Amelia was too smart to ever try such a thing. Nevertheless, she supported her daughter's adventure after the fact and sent an encouraging wire to Amelia in response.

The waiting strain showed on pilot Wilmer Stultz, who began drinking heavily. Although this problem is not mentioned in any of Amelia's subsequent writings, she tried to discourage his dependency on the bottle by taking him for long walks on the beach. Slim Gordon, the mechanic, threatened to quit if Amelia didn't send for a relief pilot, but she managed to convince him to stay on a bit longer.

The press, hounding them at all hours, added another level to the stress of the fliers. Some reporters seized on the weather delay as an indication that Amelia, when faced with the reality of the transoceanic flight, had developed a severe case of stage fright. George Putnam denied the rumor.

On June 12 the crew attempted to take off, but sea spray doused the motors and grounded them again. They learned of the successful flight of the *Southern Cross* from San Francisco to Honolulu, and on to Fiji, then the longest nonstop flight ever made. The plane was identical to the *Friendship* with the exception of the pontoons. "They made it; so could we," Amelia wrote. "Their accomplishment was a challenge."

Three takeoff attempts failed on June 17, the day the fliers finally received the word that weather was fair enough over the North Atlantic for them to proceed. On the fourth try, the *Friendship* climbed aloft, bound for Ireland with seven hundred gallons of fuel.

Just before the takeoff at 11:15 A.M., Amelia wired George Putnam the code word "Violet," alerting him of their departure. The telegram was to be sent a half hour after they were in the air. The plane, Amelia wrote, weighed about six thousand pounds empty, but its weight doubled when loaded with fuel and its crew. When they were airborne, she complained of a blinding headache, likely a symptom of her sinus condition, but managed to get some sleep.

Following a half-hour nap, Amelia wrote descriptions of coastlines and clouds in the flight log as they climbed to five thousand feet, where they passed through a snow squall. The cabin temperature dropped, but the cockpit heater spread warmth toward her and she did not feel cold. Pilot Stultz first tried to reach clearer weather by climbing, but to prevent ice from forming on the wings, he had to take the plane lower. For a good part of the journey, the *Friendship* advanced through fog, briefly breaking through the mist nearly 1,100 miles from shore, at 4,000 feet with their speed averaging 140 miles per hour. Describing the shrouded views, which had obscured the ocean for most of the flight, Amelia wrote, "I am getting housemaid's knee kneeling here at the table gulping beauty."

Thirteen hours after takeoff, she noted an altitude of ten thousand feet, but later Stultz had to make a speedy descent when the motors began coughing. He descended to three thousand feet, where he and mechanic Gordon decided the motors were running roughly due to water spray. They climbed and descended throughout the flight to find a workable altitude, but averaged three thousand feet. The two men alternated as pilot; Stultz flying four hundred miles through the inclement weather before switching places with Gordon and taking a nap.

Food and drink on this leg of the flight consisted of one thermos of black coffee and another sweetened, two and a half gallons of mineral water, oranges, egg sandwiches, chocolate, a tin of oatmeal cookies, pemmican, and malted milk tablets. The men ate sandwiches and drank coffee while Amelia ate three oranges, about six

SOME AVIATION FIRSTS

1903 December 17, Orville and Wilbur Wright, first sustained flight of a heavier-than-air craft, Kitty Hawk, North Carolina, in the Wright Flyer.

1919 June 14, Sir John Alcock and Sir Arthur Whitten Brown make the first transatlantic crossing in a Vickers Vimy biplane.

1926 May 9, Commander Richard Byrd with navigator Floyd Bennett, to the North Pole and back to Kings Bay, Spitzbergen, Norway, in the Fokker trimotor *America*.

1927 May 20, Charles A. Lindbergh, New York to Paris, first solo of Atlantic Ocean in the Ryan monoplane, *Spirit of St. Louis.*

1928 May 31–June 10, Australian pilot Charles Kingsford-Smith and crew, first flight across the Pacific Ocean, in the Fokker trimotor *Southern Cross.*

1929 Richard Byrd flies from his base at Little America, Antarctica, to the South Pole and back in the Fokker trimotor *Floyd Bennett;* first person to fly over both poles.

1931 May 23, Oklahoman Wiley Post flies around the world with navigator Harold Gatty, in *Winnie Mae,* a Lockheed Vega, in eight days, fifteen hours, and fifty-one minutes; first successful global flight.

1931 September 4, James "Jimmy" Doolittle wins the first Bendix Race in a Laird Super Solution.

1933 July 15, Wiley Post flies around the world solo in the *Winnie Mae,* using automatic pilot and radio compass direction finder, in seven days, eighteen hours, forty-nine and one-half minutes.

1935 Helen Richey, first female airline pilot for Central Airlines.

malted milk tablets, and tasted the pemmican, a type of dried meat that she did not like.

At midnight she fell asleep but awoke when Gordon tried to make radio contact with any ships in the area. When none responded, they realized their radio was dead and that they had to rely solely upon Stultz's navigational skills to keep them on course. At 8:50 A.M., Amelia made the final entries in the flight log, noting the sighting of two boats and writing, "Try to get bearing. Radio won't. One hr's gas. Mess. All craft cutting our course. Why?" The last radio contact they had been able to make had been at seven hours from Trepassey when they communicated with the British ship *Rexmore.*

Now, searching for another vessel, Stultz descended and flew over the steamer *America* but couldn't make radio contact. Amelia took a photograph of the ship, its identity unknown to the *Friendship* crew, from the open hatch of the airplane. Stultz wrote a note to the *America*'s captain, and Amelia placed it in a paper bag with an orange for weight, tossing the impromptu "bomb" through the hatch, but the drift of the airplane and the sea caused the package to land unseen in the ocean.

Stultz descended to five hundred feet, hoping to find land. Half an hour later, a fishing boat came into view, and then soon the crew saw several more. When they did see the coast and landed in the water, they found they had flown southeast of their planned destination of Ireland, arriving instead at Burry Port, Wales, on June 18 after twenty hours and forty-nine minutes in the air.

Celebrations

I n the waters of Carmarthen Bay near Burry Port, Wales, the crew of the *Friendship* looked out of their windows and saw three men working on a railroad near the beach. The men, oblivious at first to Slim Gordon's shouts and waves when he set anchor, noticed the airplane rocking in the sea and blithely returned to their job. After a few minutes some others came to the beach to gaze at the Fokker, and Gordon again shouted, asking for a boat, but his request went unanswered. Amelia dangled a towel out the front window, dismayed at the nonchalant response she received from one of the onlookers who simply removed his jacket and swung it in the air. The flight crew, unsure of their location, sat for an hour until Norman Fisher, the high sheriff of Carmarthenshire, pulled alongside in a dinghy. He took Wilmer Stultz ashore to telephone friends in Southampton while Amelia and Gordon waited in the airplane.

Later that afternoon, Captain Hilton Railey and Allen Raymond of *The New York Times*, who had earlier traveled to London, arrived by seaplane, pressing through the crowd of nearly two thousand people who had learned of the woman flier and gathered on and around the dock to see her. When Stultz returned, the *Friendship* crew decided to stay at a local hotel rather than fly the Fokker from Burry Port, where the swift tide that evening made a takeoff hazardous. They were taken ashore by boat. Amelia had Railey send short telegrams to her mother and Marion Perkins; both said simply, "Love— Amelia." Raymond later reported that when Amelia stepped on the dock, she was "nearly crushed by the anxiety of the crowd of men, women, and children to touch the hem of her flying suit, get her autograph on a slip of paper, wring her hand, and congratulate her upon her triumphant passage over the Atlantic." The extra scarf she brought along disappeared as she made her way through the mob; the red one she wore remained with her because it was tied around her neck. Six policemen formed a protective ring around her, shepherding her to the office of the Fricker Metal Company, where she made three balcony appearances to appease the public. An hour later the police escorted the crew to the hotel, where Stultz and Gordon ate dinner, then went to their rooms to enjoy a rest. Amelia stayed in her room, too excited to eat, and although tired after remaining awake for most of the past thirty hours, unable to sleep. She still needed to write the story of the crossing that George Putnam had promised to *The New York Times* and to give interviews to Railey and Raymond and other reporters, whom she greeted cheerfully despite her fatigue. In the article she said, "I never had any real doubt of the outcome." After completing her tasks, she calmed down enough to take a hot bath and sleep for six hours.

The next morning things looked brighter, and she finally took the controls of the *Friendship,* piloting the plane part of the way from Burry Port to Southampton. There, another huge crowd awaited her arrival, and two women—Amy Guest, sponsor of the flight, and Mrs. Foster Welch, the lord mayor of Southampton and the first female sheriff in England—came forward to greet her. Mr. and Mrs. Hubert Scott Payne of Imperial Airways drove Amelia to London, stopping for a moment to show her Winchester Cathedral.

In London the press barrage continued, and she faced a throng of reporters and photographers in her flower-bedecked room at the Hyde Park Hotel. At thirty, she had become a global media sweetheart. Newspapers ran banner headlines proclaiming her feat, attributing the success of the mission almost entirely to Amelia. She refused to accept the credit, naming Stultz and Gordon for any honors. On June 19, 1928, Amelia wrote in *The New York Times,* "Any praise I can give them they ought to have. You can't pile it on too thick." She insisted she had ridden along as a passenger and had not been responsible for flying the aircraft, yet the press coverage continued to credit her for the success of the crossing, and the pilot and mechanic faded from the scene. They stayed at the hotel, did some sightseeing in London, and went mostly unrecognized. Amy Guest believed the men had been well paid for their work and left them alone, but she championed her woman flier, who she realized needed some respite from the crush of people making demands upon her. Arrangements were made for her to stay at the Guests' Park Lane home, and Mrs. Guest loaned her clothes until they could go shopping at American Gordon Selfridge's department store for more suitable attire.

The newspapers carried many fabrications. Some stated she had earned degrees from Columbia University and Harvard; some wrote of her being quite wealthy while others indicated her family was poor. One report stated her father was dead. She sent Edwin a copy of that clipping for his scrapbook.

Although the press mania surprised her, the publicity delighted sponsor George Putnam. The front page of *The New York Times,* in addition to carrying the first installment of her story, carried a picture of Amelia, copyrighted by Putnam, depicting her wearing a man's tailored shirt and tie and belted leather trench coat, gazing into the distance with a serious expression on her face. *The Christian Science Monitor* proclaimed she had "the Lindy look," and she began to be called "Lady Lindy." During her stay in England she received so many congratulatory cables and requests for autographs that Hilton Railey hired four secretaries to help her tend them. President Calvin Coolidge wired, "I wish to express to you, the first woman successfully to span the North Atlantic by air, the great admiration of myself and the people of the United States for your splendid flight. Our pride in this accomplishment of our countrywoman is equaled only by our joy over her safe arrival. The courageous collaboration of the copilot, Mr. Wilmer Stultz, and Mr. Gordon likewise merit our cordial congratulations."

While in London, she attended teas and luncheons, watched a special air show, saw American Helen Wills play tennis at Wimbledon, and for the most part was placed on public display. She danced with Edward, Prince of Wales, who would later become King of England and abdicate the throne to marry the American divorcée Wallis Simpson, and was horrified when newspapers reporting the event quoted her as using the language of a country bumpkin. She met Lady Mary Heath, first woman to solo the eight thousand miles from Cape Town to London. She wanted to sell her Avro Avian biplane, and Amelia bought it, arranging credit through George Putnam, for whom she had agreed to write a book describing her Atlantic adventure. One early morning, without her hosts knowing, she left the house in a car dispatched by Lady Heath and rode to the local airfield, Croydon. There she flew in a Gypsy Moth and Heath's Avian.

She also met American-born Lady Nancy Astor, the

first woman member of Parliament, and visited her home, Cliveden, and Toynbee Hall, a settlement house and the model for Boston's Denison House, where a group of rosy-cheeked, laughing, and cheering children hailed her. Lady Astor, unlike most, wanted to learn about her social work rather than to revel in her aviation achievement. She sat between Lady Astor and Winston Churchill, also a licensed pilot, at a luncheon given by the Women's Committee of the Air League of the British Empire, and gave a brief speech. She adroitly used the opportunity to champion the abilities of women in aviation, a cause she would use her fame to promote throughout her life, and spoke of the future of aviation in the United States. She said, in part, "In our country a man may learn to fly at government expense, if he passes the requirements of the United States Army schools. I do not know of any such instruction for young women. So, until some pioneer woman has arranged better chances for young women fliers [they] must learn to fly in some private flying school." Women, she said, could find various jobs in aviation in addition to piloting, including sales work, operations of flight schools, and airfield development.

On June 28, 1928, Amelia boarded the SS *President Roosevelt*, bound for New York, with Stultz and Gordon already aboard. Captain Harry Manning, understanding her need for privacy after the frenetic ten days in England, allowed her access to the bridge deck. The Avian was transported on the ship as well, still carrying Lady

Heath's medals and including a special message from the Englishwoman, "To Amelia Earhart from Mary Heath. Always think with your stick forward."

Traveling on the ocean liner gave her a greater appreciation for the immensity of the sea. She wrote, "Eastbound the mileage had been measured in clouds, not water. There never had been adequate comprehension of the Atlantic below us."

George Putnam wired her of thirty-two invitations for appearances in various cities, and she agreed to attend several fêtes, but spent her return trip worrying over the behavior of Stultz, who had again been drinking. In London he had made inappropriate comments to the press and accidentally insulted the future king. On board ship Stultz was drunk much of the time, and Amelia despaired of sobering him up for the festivities awaiting them in America.

On July 6 the *Roosevelt* arrived in New York, serenaded by the New York Fire Department band playing "Home Sweet Home," and the mayor, Grover Whalen, clad in a tuxedo, with appropriate pomp and cirumstance, arrived on his yacht, *Macon,* to retrieve the *Friendship* crew from the liner and carry them to Battery Park, where hordes of people stood waiting for the ocean fliers. At the park a cheerful Amelia, wearing a blue crepe suit and ivory silk blouse, a nervous Stultz, and a relaxed Gordon sat on the backseat of an open car, riding on to Broadway and through the ear-numbing noise and confetti-blizzard of a ticker-tape parade. Activities in the city kept her busy until late in the night, and then three more long days crammed with appearances followed before she traveled to Boston.

She saw her mother and sister and Marion Perkins, her Denison House supervisor, briefly before being whisked away to official duties and the boisterous crowds longing to see her. Later that day, Amelia drove Amy and Muriel home to Medford in the *Yellow Peril*, but stayed at the Ritz-Carlton, probably to keep her family from being bombarded with visitors. Another round of festivities kept her busy during her two days in Boston, but she did spend some time with Sam Chapman. The couple ended their romance, and although they would continue to be good friends, she obviously could never be the traditional wife and mother he wanted to share his life.

Upon returning to New York, she participated in a radio broadcast from Madison Square Garden. Additional celebrations took place in Chicago, where Stultz disappeared before a parade held in the crew's honor. Gordon, dispatched to find him, failed to return in time for the event. George Putnam wore Stultz's leather cap, enlisted Amelia's Hyde Park classmate, Major Reed Landis, a World War I ace, to stand in for Gordon, and the men rode with her in the parade as undetected impostors. Putnam signed autographs for Stultz, then excused his absence from a dinner hosted by the mayor by fibbing about an upset stomach. No one realized the switch had been made. Amelia did not often see the men who flew with her across the ocean after that; they resumed their careers, and Stultz died about a year later when his airplane crashed as he performed aerobatics.

Amelia continued with her schedule of public appearances, visiting Altoona, Williamsburg, and Pittsburgh, Pennsylvania; and Toledo, Ohio. Offers abounded for speaking engagements and additional appearances. In Rye, New York, George Putnam and his wife, Dorothy Binney Putnam, of the crayon-making Binneys, hosted a large private party in Amelia's honor at the Westchester Biltmore, with women pilots Thea Rasche of Germany and American Ruth Nichols attending. Amelia had previously corresponded with Nichols, another F.A.I. licensed pilot who had broken her 1922 altitude record soon after it had been set, regarding forming an organization of women pilots. Putnam arranged for Amelia to stay with them in Rye while she wrote her book, *20 Hrs., 40 Mins.: Our Flight in the Friendship*. He provided in-depth editorial guidance, hoping profitable sales would follow as had been the case with the successful works of Lindbergh and Byrd, which G. P. Putnam's Sons had published previously. The book, written in three weeks with an expected September release, capitalized on the author's vibrant worldwide fame.

After such intense work and public scrutiny, Amelia needed a vacation. She decided to go "vagabonding" by flying across the country in the Avian. Characteristically secretive, she revealed her plan to Putnam, who technically owned the airplane, but only vaguely mentioned her idea to her mother in a letter without setting a firm date. However, Putnam knew a marketing advantage when he saw one, and without telling her, he alerted the press two days before she left Rye on August 29.

He accompanied her to Pittsburgh, where she damaged the Avian on landing. While taxiing, one wheel of her plane caught in an unmarked ditch, throwing the craft off balance and causing the vehicle to "ground-loop." The propeller, one wing, and the landing gear all sustained damage, but neither she nor Putnam were hurt, and both maintained the incident was not her fault. *The New York Times* carried front-page reports of the crack-up, dashing her hopes for avoiding press coverage during her trip, now delayed by two days until the Avian was repaired. Soon afterward, her plan to fly to the West Coast became generally known. The solitude she craved could be found only in the air.

Several other unfortunate mishaps marred her cross-country sojourn, wherein she stopped at Dayton, Ohio; Terre Haute, Indiana; Muskogee, Illinois; St. Louis, Missouri; Lovington, New Mexico; and Pecos, Texas. She encountered turbulence near Fort Worth and lost her navigational map when the wind blew the paper from the open cockpit. The safety pin with which she had affixed the map to her skirt had come undone. A flat tire and valve trouble in Pecos forced an emergency landing on the main street, causing a five-day delay, and the airplane had to be towed several miles for repairs at the tiresome speed of ten miles per hour, with stops every three miles to allow the plane's wheel bearings to cool. At Douglas, Arizona, the engine overheated from having been flown at high altitudes above the mountains and forced another unexpected landing. In Yuma local citizens were so eager to help that they dumped the Avian on its nose and bent the propeller. She pounded it back into shape herself, then traveled on to Glendale, California.

Everywhere she stopped she was recognized and hailed for her accomplishments. In Los Angeles she attended the National Air Races, receiving a standing ovation and garnering prodigious public adulation along with Charles Lindbergh, who was also present, for their impressive accomplishments in furthering aviation. While in the city, she visited her father and other friends, then flew as a passenger to San Francisco. There, she received a silver set of wings from the 381st Aero Squadron of the United States Army and the designation of honorary major. She treasured the wings, wearing them often and even pinning them on her gowns for formal occasions and photographs.

Her trip back to the East Coast proved to be as frustrating as her western journey. One hundred miles south of Salt Lake City the Avian's engine quit, forcing her to make a dead-stick landing in a bumpy field where she nosed over. Repairs this time took ten days, so she filled the time by lecturing at local schools and community organizations and did some sightseeing as well. She flew on to Omaha, where the *Omaha World-Herald* recorded her irritation with inconsiderate memento seekers: "Why they even cut pieces of the fabric from the wings of your machine and then ask you to autograph them! Some day a souvenir hound will carry off a vital part and there will be a crash."

By October 13 she had returned to New York, where Putnam waited with a full schedule of promotional appearances for the new book. Having conquered the Atlantic Ocean, she now added to her résumé the achievement of being the first woman to fly solo across the continent and back.

Fame

I n the months following the *Friendship* flight, Amelia wrote her book, set the transcontinental flight record, gave a hundred lectures, participated in countless interviews, and visited thirty cities. Her schedule often included two speaking engagements each day in addition to appearances at social functions, plus the necessary travel to her lectures, by train or automobile. Fourteen-hour days became typical. In January 1929 she appeared in Rochester, New York, breakfasting with the greeting committee on her arrival at the train station, then inspecting the airport and two airplane factories that morning. She served as a lunch speaker for the local advertising group, traveled to LeRoy, New York, to see the *Friendship* and its new owner, Jell-O magnate Donald Woodward, then had tea with a local couple, attended a banquet hosted by the Rochester Automobile Dealers

Association, and visited an automobile show before riding the train back to New York at ten that night.

She handled the crowds with grace, although for Amelia this was a most difficult part of her job. She didn't like to be crowded and touched by throngs of strangers, but giving lectures placed her squarely on display for the public and meant a certain amount of glad-handing. To compensate and to help quell her uneasiness, she requested a few moments of solitude before each speech to compose herself.

George Putnam taught her how to better present herself to the public, tutoring her in the art of public speaking by teaching her how to use a microphone to project her pleasant, cultured voice with its natural musical lilt and reminding her not to lower her voice at the end of sentences. He showed her how to use pointers while still facing her audience and directed her to make strong endings to her lectures. He also advised her on how to look her best in photographs, to pose to emphasize her slender figure and the unruly cluster of tawny curls that became her trademark. He criticized her choice in hats, especially the close-fitting cloches she chose, which he deemed "a public menace," and admonished her to smile with her mouth closed to hide the gap between her two front teeth.

She was always more concerned with her work than with her appearance but was not above a little feminine vanity. When in Omaha, she had asked a stage actress who appeared in a play there how she kept her creamy complexion, complaining a bit about her own sun-burned, leathery face—earned by many hours in open cockpit airplanes—and freckled nose. Her comments appeared in the newspaper, and after that, Amelia kept her beauty questions to herself. She did confide in friends that she thought her thighs looked too heavy and often chose to wear slacks to cover them. In doing so she helped set a fashion trend, along with movie stars Katharine Hepburn and Marlene Dietrich. Amelia's choice was essentially a practical one because wearing trousers allowed her more freedom when she climbed aboard an airplane, requiring a high step or two from the ground to the wing, and then another stretch to throw her leg over the cockpit window and enter the hatch. Some planes could be entered through a door in the fuselage as well, but in instances where the larger aircraft carried extra fuel tanks in the fuselage, boarding through the cockpit hatch became necessary. Smaller airplanes with open cockpits required similar agility from pilots.

In setting up her promotional schedule and managing her blossoming new career as a lecturer, Putnam made one mistake. With deft marketing skill, he included product endorsements as part of the package to promote his female flier and increase her income, but failed to recognize the demands of the public for truth in advertising. Amelia did not smoke or drink alcohol, yet she accepted $1,500 for an endorsement for Lucky Strike cigarettes, creating outrage among the public who pictured her as squeaky clean and believed proper women should not smoke, especially those who had become admirable role models for young people. She only advertised the cigarettes, along with *Friendship* pilot Wilmer Stultz and mechanic Slim Gordon, as the brand that had been used aboard the plane, but that distinction made little difference to her admirers. Other product endorsements—for Chrysler automobiles and a wool-lined leather coat with leather helmet—produced better results, and she received a blue Roadster and a coat in return for those advertisements. She had earned $12,460 for her *New York Times* articles about the *Friendship* flight and, as agreed, turned that money over to be used to defray the cost of the flight, and she gave all of the cigarette proceeds to Commander Byrd to help finance his second Antarctic flight. To rectify the Lucky Strike gaffe, Putnam planted two letters to the editor in *The New York Times,* one from Amelia to Byrd advising him of her donation and a thank-you letter from Byrd. The cigarette brouhaha cost her a chance to become an aviation editor for *McCall's* magazine, another opportunity Putnam had found for her. Otis Wiese, the editor, had received numerous letters from women upset by their heroine's endorsement and, fearing subscription and sales repercussions, withdrew his job offer. Soon after, Ray Long, editor of William Randolph Hearst's *Cosmopolitan* magazine, offered her the aviation editorship and she accepted. Her first article appeared in November 1928 and consisted mostly of information she'd earlier presented in her book about the *Friendship* flight.

Editor Long hoped to have Amelia fly to a different city each month, give a lecture to the women's club there, and write articles about these experiences, but while she could not accommodate him, she attempted to do so by hiring a ghostwriter who could handle the writing for her. However, the woman writer she spoke with, although thrilled by the idea, was pregnant and her doctor forbade her to fly. Instead, Amelia crammed her writing chores into her brief hotel stays or train rides traveling to or from other engagements, focusing on the current state of aviation—especially with regard to women. Readers were encouraged to send questions to her.

In December, when her mother visited her in New York for the holidays, Amelia made headlines by purchasing fifteen-dollar tickets for herself and her mother to ride as passengers on an air tour of the city featuring a view of the Statue of Liberty. Because passenger flights were relatively new, flight safety was of special concern to the public at that time, and Amelia penned articles, published in early 1929, explaining the strict requirements for pilots and the safety factors implemented by the aviation industry. Many people remembered the sometimes reckless early-day antics of barnstormers and stunt pilots and the resulting smashups, and avoided flying. Flying was still new enough that even minor accidents received strong news coverage and fatal crack-ups still occurred with unnerving regularity.

In one article, "Is It Safe for You to Fly?" Amelia cited the work of the two-year-old Department of Commerce in regulating flight, explaining the comprehensive process of earning a pilot's license, which included medical, written, and flight examinations, and reported that planes were licensed like automobiles. In another, "Shall You Let Your Daughter Fly?" she quoted statistics of the time showing trains were the safest mode of transportation, but equating airplanes with automobiles in safety. She also tried to reassure readers by explaining that those piloting commercial transport aircraft and their crews received intense training to help protect passengers from mishaps. She encouraged parents to fly, pointing out that firsthand experience would help them talk with their children more knowledgeably. One young woman wrote that she learned to fly without her parents' knowledge or consent, something Amelia admitted was a dangerous thing to do and believed could be avoided if parents and children felt more comfortable talking with each other about the joys of flying. "In short," she wrote, "the year 1929 is ushering in the Flying Generation."

On February 6, 1929, *The New York Times* carried the report that Amelia planned to take instruction in a Ford trimotor and intended to become a commercial pilot. In March she earned her aviator's transport pilot's license, Number 5716, becoming only the fourth woman to hold such a permit, the highest rating a pilot could attain. According to the news report, thirty-six other women held pilot licenses, rated as private pilots and limited commercial pilots. Although she had taken some private instruction, flew her Avian or any other plane offered to her whenever she could, and logged more than twice the 250 hours of airtime required to receive the license, some in the industry remained skeptical of her abilities. At the New Castle, Delaware, airport, in March 1929, she tested a Bellanca monoplane with a forty-six-foot wingspan and a Wright J5 225-horsepower engine—a much bigger ship than she was used to piloting—hoping to purchase the large plane. She flew with Elinor Smith, a younger, ambitious, and audacious pilot who had received a reprimand for flying beneath the bridges over New York's East River, but now served as a demonstration pilot for Giuseppe Bellanca's aircraft. Smith explained the Bellanca's quirk: its nose needed to be lined up slightly below the horizon indicator rather than exactly on the horizon line as was the case with most planes. Even following this instruction, Smith was disappointed in Amelia's handling of the aircraft, feeling that they "slipped and skidded all over the sky." Smith did not reveal her criticisms until many years later. A grudge she held against George Putnam for not having pushed her into the spotlight with Amelia at that time may have skewed her memory of the incident. Bellanca did not sell the airplane to Amelia, nor had he sold one to Lindbergh prior to his transatlantic flight. Lindy found another company, Ryan, to fill his need for a worthy aircraft.

Another experienced pilot believed Amelia to be competent in the cockpit. In Buffalo, New York, on March 27, 1929, following the previous day's air show, she flew a variety of planes, including a new Army trainer produced by Consolidated Aircraft. The test pilot, Leigh Wade, a World War I veteran, had flown one of the three Army Air Service planes during the first world flight in 1924 and was later interviewed by Earhart biographer Doris Rich. Of Amelia's performance that day, he said, "She was a born flier with a delicate touch on the stick."

In June 1929 she flew in her Avian to West Medford, Massachusetts, to her sister Muriel's wedding to Henry Albert Morrissey, another Great War veteran, who worked for the Boston Woven Hose and Rubber Company. She confided in the minister that she believed marrying someone required more bravery than flying in an airplane across the Atlantic.

Sometimes she needed to fly to lecture engagements or public appearances, and George Putnam and her secretary and other assistants or newsmen needed to ride along. This required a larger plane than the two-seat Avian and a second pilot so Amelia could work. (Some believed she needed the extra pilot because she could not handle the larger airplanes well.) Captain Bill Lancaster, the British pilot who had flown the first two-person flight between England and Australia, was hired as her mechanic but often flew the larger ships for her. Few people knew that Lancaster served as the pilot because, he later said, "Putnam wanted Amelia always to be given the credit and publicity for flying the aircraft."

Another article in *The New York Times,* reporting that Amelia had earned her transport pilot permit, also carried information on Paul Collins, a former airmail pilot who had been hired as the head of Transcontinental Air Transport (a predecessor of Trans World Airlines). The new airline was being formed by Clement Keys, president of Curtiss Aeroplane and Motor Company, partnered with the Pennsylvania and Santa Fe railroads. Keys eventually hired Lindbergh as T.A.T.'s chief technical adviser and hired Amelia that summer as the assistant to the general traffic manager, H. B. Clement. *The Times* quoted Clement as saying she would provide the "woman's touch" for the airline, suggesting methods to increase luxury and comfort for the female passengers. Her job also involved encouraging women, their husbands, fathers, and sons to fly. To do so, she would travel on T.A.T. planes and could promote the airline in conjunction with her own appearances.

In "Why Are Women Afraid to Fly?" published in *Cosmopolitan* in July 1929, she observed that many companies had begun buying their own airplanes to speed travel times for executives attending meetings and visiting out-of-town factories. In writing of several women who worked in aviation jobs other than pilot, she said, "I feel that if a woman should display skill comparable with a man's she would be given a comparable position in air transportation." She wrote of an existing prejudice against women in the industry, one that was not entirely unfounded due to the lack of experience and education of many women.

She also wrote of Ruth Nichols, another of the twenty-one F.A.I. licensed pilots at that time, who was organizing aviation country clubs throughout the United States offering pilots an opportunity to log hours between the time they graduated from flight schools and accepted their first flying jobs. Most pilots could not afford to purchase their own planes but needed to continue logging airtime to sharpen their skills and remain employable. In 1927, calling herself "a social worker who flies for sport," Amelia had corresponded with Nichols with the idea of forming a national women's flying organization. Nichols responded positively but waited six months for Amelia's reply, sent only weeks before her *Friendship* flight. She did apologize for being slow in responding but did not give a reason for the delay, and later, with her packed schedule following the transatlantic flight, she had not had time to pursue the matter further, though she intended to keep working on it.

The publication of the article on women's fear of flying coincided with the inaugural flight of the new airline on July 7, 1929. Although she had earned her transport license, Amelia did not serve as a pilot during the premier flight but rode as a passenger. Because air travel at night was still considered hazardous, flight at that time on T.A.T. was a complex combination of air and rail travel, and the trip from coast to coast took two days. On the first run, one airplane departed the West Coast at the same time as eastern passengers began their journey to California.

Charles Lindbergh piloted the ten-passenger T.A.T. Ford trimotor, the *City of Los Angeles,* from Glendale, California, to Winslow, Arizona. Amelia, traveling west from New York on T.A.T., met Lindbergh's plane in Winslow. Those who embarked on the transcontinental flight with her paid a ticket price equivalent to a booking on a twentieth-century Concorde but first boarded a train in New York City and rode the rails to Columbus, Ohio, where they stayed overnight. The next morning they flew from Columbus to Waynoka, Oklahoma, making stops in Indianapolis, St. Louis, Kansas City, and Wichita en route. In Waynoka they caught a night train to Clovis, New Mexico, and after their arrival in the morning, they boarded another airplane, the *City of Washington,* bound for Glendale, California, with stops in Albuquerque and Kingman and Winslow, Arizona. At Winslow they joined Lindbergh, who piloted their plane to California on July 9, 1929.

Amelia sat beside Anne Morrow, Lindbergh's new bride, during that part of the trip, and Morrow, who met Amelia for the first time in Winslow, considered her "*very* likable and very intelligent and nice and amusing." Novelist Gore Vidal, then a toddler, was a passenger aboard the inaugural flight, and recalled his eardrums felt like they were bursting when the plane suddenly lost altitude near Los Angeles. His father, Eugene Vidal, served as the assistant general manager of T.A.T., also known as "The Lindbergh Line."

Amelia remained busy, promoting the airline on the West Coast and lecturing on the Chautauqua circuit as she worked to increase her own income and help support her mother. Also, as she had done several years before, she worked so she could fly, and finally managed to buy a secondhand Lockheed Vega that summer. Lindbergh had flown it as a demonstrator for Lockheed, New York mayor Jimmy Walker sometimes used it for his transport, and the aircraft manufacturer had allowed T.A.T. to use it for test runs. She sold the Avian, eager to use her new four-passenger, 425-horsepower monoplane instead.

Daring

On a shimmering hot Sunday afternoon in August, nineteen women sat in the cockpits of their planes awaiting the signal to fly in the first Women's Air Derby. Nearly twenty thousand people thronged Santa Monica, California's Clover Field, anxious to watch the female pilots speed down the runway and lift into the air. Amelia sat in her light green Vega as the Wright Whirlwind J5 engine idled, her foot pressing the brake, the fierce sun heating the cabin to an uncomfortable temperature. Contestants lined up their planes in two horizontal rows and takeoffs would occur every minute after the official starting flag. She would be the sixth competitor to go aloft; starting positions had been calculated on the times the entrants' applications were received. The Vega, with its top speed of 135 miles per hour, and with its modern aeronautic design, was considered the fastest ship entered.

She gripped the control that powered November Charlie 31 Echo, the thirty-sixth Vega built by Lockheed, and tried to shake off thoughts of disappointment in her first Vega's performance. The secondhand airplane she had purchased earlier hadn't passed its routine safety inspection. At the Lockheed plant, test pilot Wiley Post had pronounced it unsafe to fly, and the company had replaced it with this newer one. She rubbed her sweat-moistened hands on her breeks, recalling her first flight in that ship. The altimeter had failed, leaving her to estimate her altitude by taking readings from the fuel mixture and carburetor controls instead. She glanced at the instrument panel, hoping this one would serve her well through the next eight days of the cross-country race. After adjusting her map she mentally reviewed the route to San Bernardino, the first stop, less than one hundred miles away. She had been taking some private instruction when she could fit it in, hoping to hone her skills in preparation for this event.

Some of the contestants had arrived shortly before the race's scheduled 2:15 P.M. start, flying themselves to the field and then preparing for another takeoff soon after. Amelia had flown in a Goodyear blimp with Irene Maddux, wife of Jack Maddux, one of Clement Keys's partners in T.A.T. Before resting with the Madduxes at their home at Lake Arrowhead over the weekend, she had worked at promoting the derby as well as tending to her own tasks, even speaking about the race on the radio when Maddux hosted a dinner for several of the derby contestants aboard one of his transport planes. The competition was part of the National Air Races in Cleveland, the derby's final stop, and was being managed by Cliff Henderson, director of the National Air Races and Aeronautical Exposition. Entrants in the race, dubbed the "Powder Puff Derby" by cowboy humorist Will Rogers in his opening remarks, competed for an $8,000 purse offered by the Santa Monica Bay Exchange Club, sponsor of the event. The derby was to be the first race of its kind in the world.

Cliff Henderson fired a pistol in Cleveland, its cracking sound carried over the radio in Santa Monica, to start the derby. One after another, the airplanes—low-winged and high-winged, sporty biplanes and monoplanes, some open cockpits and some cabin transports like her Vega—began lifting into the air with efficient regularity. The variety of aircraft gave spectators a taste of the diverse models built by manufacturers, displaying several Beech Travel Airs, Curtiss Robins, a Monocoupe, Rearwin, Sparton, Fleet, Swallow, Moth, Waco, Golden Eagle, American Eagle, and Alexander Bullet. The competition had been divided into two classes with the lighter planes with up to 510 cubic feet displacement engines in a separate category from the heavier ones (up to 800 cubic feet displacement) like the Vega, six of which contained the same powerful engine as Amelia's airplane. The women who entered came from several states, and two competitors—Thea Rasche and Jessie Maude "Chubby" Miller—came in from Germany and New Zealand, respectively. Each of the contestants flew alone and would stop at sixteen sites in eight days.

The fifth plane sped down the runway and into the southeastern haze. Amelia taxied into position. Ahead of her, the starter dropped the red flag ten times, hesitated for a second, then dropped the red flag with a white one. She opened the throttle and released the brake. The Vega hurtled down the runway, then suddenly felt lighter as its tail rose and the wind beneath its wing lifted the wooden airplane and its pilot into the air. As she went aloft, a magneto switch shorted out. She looked behind to watch for the next plane, then banked the Vega and began circling the field at a safe distance, waiting for the rest of the competitors to takeoff so she could land and get the faulty switch repaired. The smooth start she'd planned had not materialized; she could only hope that the other fliers had better luck. The extra minutes spent fixing the switch would be added on to her elapsed time; she'd have to make up those lost minutes somewhere along the route.

In San Bernardino other mishaps occurred. Opal Kunz of New York ground-looped her Travel Air, wrecking the plane's undercarriage. Such accidents occurred often in taildraggers on takeoffs or landings when the airplane's tail, where most of the weight of the craft was located, swerved and tried to overtake the nose of the ship. If the unexpected ground spin was severe enough, as Kunz discovered, the landing gear crumpled, causing the propeller, wing, and undercarriage to strike the ground with disastrous results. Fellow contestant Mary Von Mack of Detroit had turned back to Santa Monica, landing in Montebello, dashing her chances in the race but planning to follow the route anyway. Chubby Miller, the New Zealand pilot who had flown with Bill Lancaster on the England-to-Australia flight, had been delayed because a mechanic mistakenly put oil in her fuel tank.

Contestants felt edgy because of rumors that their planes might be targets for tampering. Crowds gathered around to view the women and their airplanes, clamoring for autographs, ignorant of the damage they could do by pushing forward near the fragile birds. Thea Rasche of Germany had received a note prior to the race warning her to beware of sabotage and had made race officials aware of this potential danger. The officials planned a stop at Calexico, California, but met with resistance from some of the pilots who had put down there just a week earlier and thought the site unsuitable for landings in heavy airplanes. The discussion took place until after midnight, when the officials relented and chose an alternate place, leaving little time for the contestants to revise their routes and prepare mentally for the next stopover, Yuma, Arizona, before getting some rest. That location was not ideal, either; sandy conditions on the landing strip there would challenge the pilots' skills. Takeoff from San Bernardino, originally scheduled for 8:00 A.M., had been moved ahead to 6:00 A.M.

Louise Thaden of Pittsburgh, Pennsylvania, who flew a Travel Air, recalled beginning the day in San Bernardino on a scant two hours' sleep. She wrote, "On the airport hollow-eyed, we shivered in the chill. Wisps of grey fog clung in thin strings to the valley floor. The runway was still ankle deep in dust." The dust severely limited visibility, making takeoffs hazardous. As each plane headed skyward, a wake of whirling dirt followed, and Thaden said she couldn't even see the end of the runway when she took off.

On the second leg of the journey, the women headed across the desert, each carrying a can of tomatoes to sustain them in the event of a forced landing in the parched country. They arrived in Yuma at nearly 9:00 A.M., with a noon departure scheduled for their next overnight stop in Phoenix. On landing, Amelia struck sand toward the end of the runway and nosed over, damaging her propeller. Derby contestants displayed their sportsmanship by waiting an extra hour and a half for the repairs to be made so that she would not be penalized for the additional time.

Thaden recalled being flagged for her departure too soon and nearly hitting the plane ahead of her because of the swirling dust that obscured her vision. Between Yuma and Phoenix, her imagination began to get the best of her, causing her to worry whether the engine was misfiring and to gaze below and pick out possible forced landing spots. She attributed her wandering mind to the heat and desolation of "the brown barren drabness of desert" and wrote, "Violent updrafts followed by equally vicious downdrafts threw the plane into awkward positions until it might have been a toy in giant hands flung about in devilish mischievous glee; or a puppet on a string." She flew into Phoenix in the lead.

Florence "Pancho" Lowe Barnes, an heiress from Pasadena, who earned her nickname from working on the crew of a boat suspected of running guns to Mexico, encountered trouble on this leg of the trip when she flew off course and followed railroad tracks only to discover it was the wrong railroad. She landed near some small buildings on a farm, discovered that the occupants did not speak English, and realized that she had set down in Mexico. Because her plane could have been confiscated by customs officials there, she made a hasty takeoff and found her way back.

Other contestants suffered setbacks that seemed to underscore the rumors of sabotage. One competitor dropped out of the race because she suspected the broken wing braces on her plane had been doused with corrosive acid. Her husband, who helped her investigate the damage, agreed and advised her to quit. German flier Thea Rasche and endurance flight record holder Bobbi Trout, of Los Angeles, a twenty-three-year-old factory test pilot who held a transport license, made forced landings because of dirt in their gas tanks and wrecked their landing gears.

Worst of all, twenty-five-year-old Marvel Crosson, a

commercial pilot who had recently set a new women's altitude record at 23,996 feet, did not arrive in Phoenix. Local ranchers reported seeing her plane dive and disappear in a thick stand of cottonwood trees near the Gila River, but darkness hampered the search for her. Her body was found the next day, parachute unopened, a short distance from the airplane. The tragedy saddened everyone and threatened the existence of the derby when newspapers carried headlines proclaiming women incapable of air racing. Contestants and officials agreed that the competition should continue.

Thaden recalled, "Amelia aptly expressed our general feeling. 'Marvel Crosson left a challenge to the women of the Derby and there is certainly no aftermath of fear among us.'"

As the race progressed, the women grew increasingly tired but kept the competitive edge; their flying times remained close, sometimes within minutes of each other. Their schedule consisted of rising before dawn for early morning takeoffs, then flying for about two hours to the next stop. There, they would sign autographs and visit with spectators while trying to watch their planes to protect them from the curious public, feeling much the same anxiety as Lindbergh had when he landed in Paris in 1927 and feared the pressure of the welcoming crowd would crack the fragile fuselage of the *Spirit of St. Louis*. (People anxious to touch the racers' aircraft, still a novelty two years after Lindy's famous flight, even poked holes in the fabric wings with pencils.)

Following the autograph sessions, the women were whisked off to a luncheon, often in the nearby town, and returned after lunch to take flight again during the afternoon. At some stops, amenities such as cold cream, soap, towels, combs, and powder were provided for the pilots. In Douglas, Arizona, and El Paso, Texas, military personnel took charge of the airplanes, allowing the weary pilots a brief respite and well-deserved rest. In the evenings the fliers made certain their planes were well cared for at the fields, and then dressed up and attended banquets held in their honor. Following the requisite chicken dinners, competitors usually checked their planes again before retiring, often as late as 1:30 A.M.

By the time they reached Tulsa, just fifteen racers remained. In Fort Worth, Margaret Perry of Los Angeles withdrew; she'd felt ill when she began the competition and discovered in the Texas hospital she had typhoid fever. Pancho Barnes, the heiress with the colorful background, suffered a nasty crack-up in Pecos, Texas, where spectators parked their cars too near the narrow landing strip. She clipped the right wings on her Travel Air when they sheared the top from a Chevrolet automobile, but no one was injured. Blanche Noyes, an actress from Cleveland, arrived there shaking and with burned hands. Flying at three thousand feet above Texas, she discovered a fire in the cockpit caused by a carelessly thrown cigarette and had the presence of mind to land in the mesquite and sagebrush, throw sand on the blaze, and return to the air.

Thunderstorms threatened between Tulsa and Wichita, and leader Louise Thaden described the feel of raindrops hitting her face in the open cockpit as "the stabs of a million needles." In East St. Louis, Illinois, her mechanic discovered that someone had filed the breaker points on her magnetos but was able to make repairs at the last minute. On this sixth day of the race, exhausted contestants had grown used to the routine of melancholy morning starts in gray dawns and the late-night checks of their airplanes. Many of them had perpetually sore feet from pressing the rudder bars during flight.

Columbus, Ohio, was the final stop before the end of the race in Cleveland. There, competitor Ruth Nichols of Rye, New York, one of the first three women in the nation to earn her transport license, crashed into a steamroller parked near the end of the runway, causing her Rearwin to cartwheel twice and land on its top. Amelia, preparing for takeoff, stopped the Vega, climbed from the cockpit, and ran to help Ruth, losing her position in the takeoff slate. Nichols had turned off the ignition switch, preventing the gasoline from catching fire, and climbed from the wreckage unhurt but out of the race. The two women had engaged in an unspoken private competition during the event, and both regretted Nichols's unexpected ending. Once assured Ruth was unharmed, Amelia climbed into the Vega and flew to Cleveland.

Louise Thaden arrived first, with the fastest elapsed

time of twenty-one hours and nineteen minutes, and received $3,600. Gladys O'Donnell of Long Beach, California, followed, just twenty-two minutes behind, earning $1,950. Amelia, an hour and forty-five minutes behind Thaden, approached the field with open throttle, being careful not to stall the Vega by losing speed, but struggling with the landing. Elinor Smith watched as she sped down the runway, braking furiously, and earning third place and a prize of $875. Smith admired Amelia's performance, believing she hadn't accumulated enough airtime in larger planes to have flown as well as she did. Her fellow pilot's weary expression when she threw open the cockpit and climbed out revealed the tension Amelia had felt during the landing, and Smith described her performance as "gut courage that transcended the sanity of reasoning."

Eighteen thousand spectators spilled onto the field in Cleveland, as eager to see the pilots as those at the sixteen other towns they had flown to, and the onlookers clambered on and around the airplanes, some even standing on the wings and walking across them. Despite the difficulty in controlling the crowds, and even with all the accidents, the derby had promoted flying, had shown that women were capable pilots, and as Amelia later noted, the competition had the highest percentage of finishers, male or female, in any cross-country race to that date. In an interview for *The Woman's Journal,* she said, "The derby, I feel, added considerably to our flying knowledge and at the same time served to increase public interest and confidence in women in aviation."

Several of the racers, including Amelia, competed in special events at the National Air Races, but she could not match her bravado performance in the derby. In a closed-course race, she flew a Great Lakes biplane and urged Blanche Noyes to join her in the competition. Neither woman had flown that make of aircraft before, and although Noyes finished third, Amelia did not have the skill to make the necessary tight turns at the pylons and was disqualified. The next day, Frank Hawks, the man who had taken Amelia for her first airplane ride, organized "The Famous Motored Pilots' Derby," in association with the National Glider Association, featuring prominent fliers piloting gliders. Amelia tried a turn without having gained enough airspeed, causing her glider to spin. She managed to pull out of the spin before she crashed but landed hard—and right in front of the grandstand.

Speed

ollowing the National Air Races, several women pilots gathered in Amelia's hotel room to chat about forming a new national organization. Women who worked for the Curtiss-Wright Flying Service in New York, including derby contestants Opal Kunz and Neva Paris, had also warmed to the idea of a new club but hadn't communicated their enthusiasm about the idea to Amelia and her Rye neighbor Ruth Nichols until this casual discussion. The group would focus on promoting women in aviation, and several women, working with Amelia, formulated a plan. Ruth Nichols; Gladys O'Donnell of Long Beach, California, who finished second in the Women's Air Derby; Louise Thaden, winner of the event; and Phoebe Omlie, the woman pilot who had been one of the first three females to earn a transport license and who won the light-class division in the race, outlined membership qualifications and organizational goals. When the discussion turned to forcing equality with male pilots by racing them and using the same airplanes, some of the women balked. The men's racers were basically flying gasoline tanks, heavier and harder to handle than the planes the women were used to, and even more dangerous. Because of the disagreement, Bellanca demonstration pilot Elinor Smith and a few others declined to join the proposed organization.

Letters of invitation signed by Neva Paris and three others were issued to the 117 licensed women pilots throughout the nation. Eighty-six pilots responded, and on November 2, 1929, at Curtiss Airport, New York, twenty-six women from six states, many arriving by car and train because of bad weather, met in an airplane hangar to formally organize the new association. While enjoying tea served from a toolbox on wheels, and speaking over the din of the mechanics revving motors as they worked nearby, the women decided membership would be open to any woman with a pilot's license. The group would provide camaraderie as well as a central location for files on women in aviation. Suggestions for names made little improvement over Will Rogers's moniker of "powder puff" for the air derby: "Gadflies," "Climbing Vines," "Homing Pigeons," "Moon Calves," "Air Dames," "Lady Birds," "Queens High." Amelia, who had been quiet during most of the meeting, suggested that the club be named with the number of charter members.

The women agreed; the number would be based on the amount of acceptances they received. Several late replies arrived increasing the original eighty-six to ninety-nine. The club first used "99s" as their name and later changed it to the Ninety-Nines, Inc. At that meeting, Amelia earned respect from her sister pilots—many of whom were more experienced than she—because even though she was better known, she was willing to listen and learn rather than foist her ideas upon them.

The high-spirited women of the Ninety-Nines, although each had in common promoting aviation, confronted some difficulties in settling on officers to direct the organization. Opal Kunz agreed to act as president until formal elections were held. The Ninety-Nines remained informal, producing a newsletter and hosting annual meetings to keep communication lines open between members. Acting secretary Neva Paris was killed in January 1930, when her plane crashed in Georgia as she traveled to air races in Florida, and Louise Thaden took over the secretarial duties with Blanche Noyes, the Cleveland actress and flier as treasurer. Amelia was elected president that same year.

Following the organizational meeting in November, 1929, Amelia set another record, this time a speed record for a one-mile distance, although the feat went unrecognized for a year. She had flown her Vega to Los Angeles a few days after the Ninety-Nines meeting, accompanied by Norah Alstulund, her new secretary. The two women stayed as houseguests of T.A.T. owners Jack and Irene Maddux, and Amelia tended some of her airline duties. While in California, she visited the Lockheed plant in Burbank, anxious to find a new airplane, studying all the models and their specifications and test-flying each. On November 22 she broke the women's speed record of 156 miles per hour set by Louise Thaden. Amelia flew an Executive SF Lockheed, a demonstrator model owned by Detroit Aircraft Corporation, taking four laps with the fastest speed of 197.80. The National Aeronautic Association rules had been followed, and an official timer clocked the speed, but the association did not accept the record because they did not recognize one-mile courses, following instead the Fédération Aéronautique Internationale rules that the shortest course of three kilometers was for world maximum speed records only.

By this time she'd set her sights on another Vega, one built prior to the model she piloted in the derby. It had been used as a demonstrator, and she flew it while in California but the plane was not registered to her until February 18, 1930. While searching for her own aircraft, she had ridden as a passenger in a new Lockheed Sirius, a more expensive model than she could afford, and recently purchased by Charles Lindbergh. Amelia rode in Lucky Lindy's plane before he had even flown in it.

The Lindberghs visited the Madduxes during this time, and Anne Lindbergh wrote to her sister about Amelia: "She is the most amazing person—just as tremendous as C. [Charles], I think. It startles me how much alike they are in breadth. C. doesn't realize it, but he hasn't talked to her as much. She has the clarity of mind, impersonal eye, coolness of temperament, balance of a scientist. Aside from that, I like her."

On January 9 Amelia left for New York, flying her new airplane with Norah Alstulund as passenger. They stopped at Albuquerque the first night, then returned the next day when a severe winter storm blocked their path to Las Vegas. Since she had lecture commitments and magazine article deadlines to meet, she dared not wait out the bad weather and left her Vega in New Mexico, returning home with Norah by train.

Between meeting her public appearance obligations and working to promote the Ninety-Nines, Amelia tried to help her parents. Amy was then living in West Medford, Massachusetts, with Muriel, who was expecting her first child and coping with a difficult marriage. Amelia kept in touch with her mother through hasty though fairly frequent correspondence, voicing her concern about her sister's situation. Her father, Edwin, was very ill, living in California, and Amelia had visited him and his wife, Helen, at their home in Eagle Rock near Los Angeles. Because he was so frail, he worried about not being able to keep his mortgage payments current, so Amelia paid the $2,000 debt and kept the title of the house in her name. She arranged a life tenancy document so that the property would be left to her father in the event of her death and if he died, to his wife. Even though her own financial security was at risk at a time when the nation was confronting the Great Depression, she also wanted to tend to her mother's financial needs as much as possible.

Amelia earned the most income from lectures, receiving additional revenue from magazine articles and book royalties, and when she arrived in New York, she sent Amy $100 and advised her that the sum would be sent to her regularly from the bank. She had invested her own earnings in stocks and bonds and signed over the annual income to her mother, as well as setting aside a $1,000 bond for her that could be cashed at any time. Keeping her mind on the future, which for any pilot contained the distinct possibility of an accidental death, she purchased life insurance from the National Air Pilots' Association and named Amy as beneficiary. She explained that she was living frugally by splitting expenses with Norah, who was rooming with her in New York, and told her mother not to worry because she had met her own financial needs without difficulty.

In February she headed west to pick up the Vega, and later that month flew in an exhibition in St. Louis with some other famous pilots—Clarence Chamberlin, who had soloed the Atlantic after Lindbergh; Frank Hawks, the barnstormer who gave Amelia her first airplane ride; Elinor Smith, the daring young woman who had flown beneath New York's bridges and was now a demonstrator pilot for Bellanca Aircraft, and James "Jimmy" Doolittle, an Army test pilot and war veteran who would later lead the great bombing raid on Tokyo during World War II.

She also observed maneuvers on the aircraft carrier *Lexington* at Norfolk, Virginia, keeping her name before the public to help her earn more opportunities for lectures and magazine articles. From April through June, she made numerous appearances, often speaking twice per day to different groups in the same town, and flying to her destinations—Detroit, Kansas City, Indianapolis, Chicago, Philadelphia.

Amelia continued to pursue Fédération Aéronautique Internationale record classification for women. She believed that women should earn their records through competitions with men, but realized that women did not have adequate air experience and pushed instead for recognition of special record categories for women and for their right to compete for world records.

In late June and early July, she flew another Vega, this one borrowed from Lockheed, at the Grosse Isle Airport in Detroit, and set three records that would go unrecognized by the F.A.I. for a year. On June 25, 1930, she flew one hundred kilometers at 174.897 miles per hour, achieving the women's world speed record with no load carried. That same day, carrying a payload of five hundred kilograms, she clocked 171.438 miles per hour over one hundred kilometers, setting the women's world speed record. Ten days later, she set the women's world speed record over a three-kilometer course at 181.18 miles per hour. She had requested, received, and followed National Aeronautic Association rules, but had to correspond frequently with the F.A.I. throughout the year to convince the organization to recognize her achievements.

Other women were as vocal as Amelia in trying to encourage females to take up flying, including Margery Brown, the only woman taught to fly by William Winston, Lindbergh's flight instructor. Calling flight "a symbol of freedom from limitation," Brown wrote in the June issue of *Pictorial Review* that "every woman who overcomes a limitation has gained a measure of freedom, not alone for herself, but for her sex. A victory for one woman is a victory for all."

In early August, Amelia and four others refused to fly in the Women's Air Derby, planned as part of the National Air Races held in Chicago. Louise Thaden, the previous winner of the derby; Blanche Noyes, the actress and former derby contestant; Elinor Smith, an airplane demonstration pilot; and Ruth Nichols, who had crashed before completing the derby, withdrew from the event with Amelia. *The New York Times* reported the fliers disagreed with the engine-size restriction dictated by the management of the race. The ruling would have required the women to fly in planes smaller than they were used to piloting. Amelia said that she could not afford to provide another craft and the new regulation would disqualify her Vega. The newspaper stated, "Miss Earhart explained that the women have outgrown the small craft used in last year's race and take great pride in their ability to perform to higher standards of piloting ability." Two Army pilots and a flight surgeon were also supposed to fly along with the women in case of emergencies and the women refused this help unless the men received the same attention.

In August 1930 Amelia began work for a new airline, the New York, Philadelphia, and Washington Airway, the first shuttle service to fly between those cities. Her friend, Eugene Vidal, formerly at T.A.T., asked her to become the vice president in charge of public relations of the new line. The prominent Philadelphia socialites, brothers Nicholas and Charles Ludington, provided financial backing for the venture and later allowed the airline to be called The Ludington Line. Vidal, a former Army flier, the first aeronautics instructor at West Point, and son-in-law of Senator T. P. Gore of Oklahoma, was joined by Paul Collins, a former airmail pilot who had also worked for T.A.T. Their mission was to begin a new, convenient service of flights on the hour, with ten round-trips daily. By providing speedier service than the other forms of available transportation, they hoped to attract a good portion of the ninety-six thousand weekly commuters between New York and Philadelphia and the seventy-nine thousand who traveled by car or train between New York and Washington. Operations began on September 1, 1930, and Amelia flew on the second Stinson trimotor departing from New York that day. During its first ten days of operation, the airline carried 1,557 passengers and, she reported, women had purchased almost half of the tickets.

Problems arose. The cabins were not pressurized and

temperatures never seemed to even out, being too warm or too cold, and this, combined with the greasy odor of exhaust fumes contained in the closed cabin, often caused travelers to experience airsickness. Passengers also had to become accustomed to weight restrictions on luggage so that the ten-seat Stinsons would not be overloaded. And since the airplanes flew at top speeds of only about one hundred fifty miles per hour and at low altitudes, about ten thousand feet, air turbulence created some bumpy rides and increased the queasiness felt by many. Hard-boiled eggs and saltine crackers were served, as studies had shown that these foods were least likely to create airsickness problems, but the snacks did not always eliminate nausea.

In her duties for the airline, Amelia recalled the transport of a canary from New York to Washington and of a pony that had been ferried on the line by allowing him room for two seats and positioning him partly in the aisle. A New York florist sent a bouquet of violets to a client in Washington, but the flowers, stowed next to the heater, wilted before they arrived. A similar fate awaited ice cream sent from New York to a Philadelphia luncheon. The dessert arrived on time in Philadelphia but was mistakenly left on the airplane and sent on to Washington before reaching its proper destination that evening.

Later in September, she flew to Los Angeles as a passenger on T.A.T., and visited her father and Helen for several days. He had been failing rapidly, unable to eat as his throat cancer progressed. She had earlier guaranteed payments for required blood transfusions, and now, seeing his deteriorating condition, she helped him and Helen by paying some of her father's debts and making funeral arrangements before returning to New York. On September 23, when she arrived in Tucson on T.A.T., she received the news that his death occurred about eight hours after her departure.

She continued on to New York and there decided to fly her Vega to a lecture scheduled for September 25 in Norfolk, Virginia. Grief over her father's death affected her mental attitude, but potholes in the landing strip created physical hazards, and when she braked to avoid one, the latch on the cockpit door gave way. Since the door was part of the pilot's seat, she toppled backward. Carl Harper, the pilot from Detroit Aircraft Company with whom she'd test-flown the Vega, was riding in the back and hurried to her, disrupting the balance of the airplane and throwing the nose forward. Harper suffered a broken finger, Amelia a scalp wound. Local doctors created a bandage that resembled a turban, and a pretty pin from a friend dressed it up enough that Amelia gave her lecture to the Norfolk-Portsmouth Traffic Club.

She downplayed the seriousness of the accident when she wrote to her mother a few days later, but the Vega had been so badly damaged that it had to be sent to Detroit to be rebuilt.

Spirals

George Palmer Putnam led a fast-paced life, scouting the United States and Europe for new authors to expand the line of his family publishing business, G. P. Putnam's Sons. He had joined the firm in 1919, following the deaths of his father in 1917 and his brother the following year. He returned from Army service to take the vacant position in the company, working with his elderly uncles, and brought with him a stellar background for a young man of thirty-two, having edited and published a newspaper and served as mayor of Bend, Oregon, and secretary to an Oregon governor. He loved adventure, and some of his most notable publishing successes for Putnam's described adventure firsthand—such books as Commander Richard Byrd's *Skyward*, the story of his North Pole expedition, and Charles Lindbergh's *We*, chronicling his lone flight from New York to Paris. Putnam had even recruited his twelve-year-old son, David Binney Putnam, into the company and after the two accompanied explorer William Beebe on his expedition to the Sargasso Sea and the Galapagos Islands, he wrote *David Goes Voyaging,* first in a series of boys' adventure books. Dan Streeter, the official expedition historian, called Putnam "a Publisher with chronic wanderlust."

While he also had a reputation as a shrewd businessman, not everyone appreciated his methods. Commander Byrd and Putnam fell out over a disagreement involving donations for his expeditions. Putnam believed that Byrd should repay the donors by splitting his profits, offering the supporters up to a quarter of the total receipts as a goodwill gesture to strengthen potential donations in future ventures. The adventurer thought otherwise, believing that the person who takes the risks should reap the rewards. The men came to a parting of the ways over this dispute.

The forty-one-year-old publisher was married to Dorothy Binney Putnam, and in addition to their son David, the couple had a nine-year-old boy, George Palmer Putnam, Jr. However, their seventeen-year relationship had begun to fray, and in 1928, searching for a woman to take the place of Amy Phipps Guest, the sponsor of the *Friendship* Atlantic crossing, Putnam met Amelia Earhart. He had hoped to find a woman who resembled Charles Lindbergh to add to the promotion of the flight, and he discovered, in Amelia, that remarkably similar, fresh-faced appearance and a likable, gracious personality.

Hilton H. Railey, the newspaperman whom Putnam had dispatched to call on Amelia, later wrote, "Her resemblance to Colonel Lindbergh was so extraordinary that I couldn't resist the impulse to ask her to remove her hat. She complied, brushing back her naturally tousled, windswept hair, and her laugh was infectious. . . . Most of all I was impressed by the poise of the boyish figure at my desk. There was warmth and dignity in her manner, her speech." He believed her to be the "sublimation" of the American woman.

Amelia's blue-gray eyes sparkled with exuberance, especially when she spoke of flying, and her mellow voice warmed with her passion about the topic. Her cap of curly light brown hair set off a delicate oval face, mostly set in a composed and somewhat serious expression, and her gap-toothed smile added to her charm. Her five-foot–eight-inch height was emphasized by her willowy build, and her elegant, slender fingers seemed too dainty to operate the controls of airplanes.

Putnam escorted Amelia to his New York office for the interview with attorney David Layman and Amy Guest's brother, John Phipps, and even though the men were impressed by the self-assured young woman, she was unimpressed with the dashing, bespectacled publisher. She later confided to her supervisor at Denison House, the Boston settlement house, that she had found him to be "a fascinating man," but felt dismayed when he rushed her back onto the return train to Boston as if pleased to be rid of her.

Putnam was quoted in *The New York Times* following her ride in the *Friendship*, commending her "indomitable will and extraordinary courage," and saying it was her "determination more than anything else which one must admire in contemplating this fresh achievement in aviation." Upon her return to the States, the keen promoter became her business manager. He seized the opportunity for additional marketing of the woman now known as "Lady Lindy," contracted with her to write a book about her *Friendship* experience, and to protect Amelia from the distraction of her adoring public, invited her to stay at his home in Rye, New York, while working on the manuscript. He hoped to follow up the success of Lindbergh's *We* with another aviation autobiography. (Lindbergh's ghostwriter had completed his manuscript at the Putnam home in Rye before the famous aviator decided he'd rather write the book himself.) The arrangement apparently suited Dorothy Putnam, and in a gesture of gratitude, Amelia dedicated her book to her hostess.

The two women were friends at first. Dorothy Putnam had even ridden along as a passenger in Amelia's Avro Avian and enjoyed the attention heaped on her husband as a result of the young woman's daring adventure. Interviewed by *The New York Times* on the flight, she described Amelia as "most extraordinarily cool and self-possessed." But Dorothy's marriage was on rocky ground; she had requested a separation eight years before, and now, while her husband had been working with his new client, she had been seeing a younger man. Putnam skipped the annual summer vacation with his wife to the Double Dee Ranch in Meeteetse, Wyoming, blaming his stringent work schedule, including overseeing Amelia's business and helping her to complete her book, finished in mid-August. By that time, rumors were circulating about a romance between the publisher and his lady pilot. Dorothy grew bitter toward Amelia yet attended events honoring her, even participating in a submarine diving expedition with Amelia that attracted huge press coverage.

Putnam continued with his other publishing duties, enjoyed the company of many celebrities, including humorist Will Rogers, artist Rockwell Kent, and novelist Dorothy Canfield Fisher, but always had time for Amelia. In August 1929 he lunched with her during the Cincinnati stopover of the Women's Air Derby, flying there in a Great Lakes trainer with pilot Bill Lancaster, who had successfully flown from England to Australia. His friend and copilot on that trip, "Chubby" Miller, joined them for lunch. The men took off, ahead of the women pilots, but they experienced engine trouble and crash-landed in a cornfield. Soon after, the racers flew overhead but failed to notice the wreck below although the men waved at them. He later asked Amelia if she would have stopped had she seen them. She teased, "You wouldn't have wanted me to drop out of the race."

They communicated mainly through letters. Putnam wrote often, and Amelia replied by scribbling notes on the margins of his letters to her. Although their temperaments differed—she was unruffled and focused, while he was prone to angry outbursts and preferred to juggle many projects simultaneously—they shared a love of the outdoors and a thirst for new adventures.

Dorothy Binney Putnam filed for divorce on the grounds of his "failure to provide," and when the final papers were served on Putnam in London in December 1929, reporters flocked to Amelia to find out if she planned to marry him. She told them no, insisting that he was her publisher and business colleague. She also wrote to her mother to make clear she had no such plans. Dorothy Putnam remarried within a month of the divorce and moved to Florida with the couple's two sons. She and her ex-husband had agreed upon joint custody.

Although Putnam recalled having proposed at least twice, and her sister Muriel counted six times, Amelia kept him at bay. She viewed marriage as confining, writing to a friend in 1930: "I am still unsold on marriage. I don't want *anything,* all of the time. . . . I think I may not ever be able to see marriage except as a cage until I am unfit to work or fly or be active—and of course I wouldn't be desirable then."

Putnam's uncle, George Haven Putnam, president of G. P. Putnam's Sons, died in February 1930, and a family squabble over ownership of the business resulted in

Putnam selling his shares. On his departure, *Time* magazine described him as "a man with a dangerous combination of literary ability, business acumen, and energy." He was quite frugal and known to have a hot although not violent temper. In August 1930 he joined Brewer and Warren publishers as vice president and wrote a biography of balloonist Salomon August André, dedicating it to "a favorite aeronaut about to embark on a new adventure." He had fallen hard for Amelia and continued to attempt to court her. His enjoyment of the limelight played into his marketing of his favorite woman pilot and caused reporters to dub him "the lens louse," since, whenever they sought a photograph of Amelia, Putnam found a way to be included and often interjected his own opinions into her interviews.

When he proposed to her in October, she finally accepted. He obtained the marriage license on November 8, 1930, in Noank, Connecticut, and the town clerk confirmed it to *The New York Times*, although Amelia denied the wedding speculation, saying, "Sometime in the next fifty years I may be married." Her reluctance to admit the obvious stemmed from her irritation at Putnam, the eternal promoter, for leaking the information to the press. She wanted their marriage plans to be secret. Though speculation continued as to when the wedding would occur and some even wondered whether the vows would take place at all, Putnam received a waiver on the waiting period required by the state of Connecticut, and the couple patched up their disagreement.

Amelia took a radical stance on her upcoming marriage. On the day of the ceremony, dressed in a simple brown suit, gloves, and shoes, she presented her business manager–fiancé with a document that many prospective grooms would have found colossally disturbing. The letter, indicative of a business agreement rather than setting any romantic tone for their partnership, did hurt the groom's feelings, and Putnam, whom she called "G.P.," said it was "a sad little letter, brutal in its frankness, but beautiful in its honesty" as he concurred with her requests. Her willingness to marry him was, he said, "an heroic decision," and they had previously discussed the issues of what amounted to a prenuptial agreement. She wrote, "You must know again my reluctance to marry, my feeling that I shatter thereby chances in work which means so much to me. I feel the move just now as foolish as anything I could do." Further, she stated, "In our life together I shall not hold you to any medieval code of faithfulness to me, nor shall I consider myself bound to you similarly." She also alerted him to the fact that she might need "someplace where I can go to be myself now and then, for I cannot guarantee to endure at all times the confinement of even an attractive cage." She ended the note by asking that he release her from the relationship in a year if they weren't happy, promising to do her best to succeed, and signed the letter "A.E."

Their simple, private, five-minute wedding took place at his mother's home in Noank on Saturday, February 7, 1931. Judge Arthur Anderson, a friend of the family, officiated, with Frances Putnam, George's mother, and his uncle, Charles Faulkner, and the judge's son, Robert, as witnesses, and two black cats in attendance as well. They took no honeymoon trip but instead went away for a quiet weekend together and then reported for work as usual on Monday morning. Despite Amelia's request for secrecy, G.P. had his secretary release the details of their wedding to the press following the ceremony.

Amy Earhart, who disliked Putnam, had objected to the marriage because he was ten years older than her daughter and divorced. After the ceremony, Amelia, who had decided to keep her maiden name for business purposes, wired her sister, "Over the broomstick with G.P. today. Break the news gently to Mother."

She later wrote of her marriage, "Ours has been a contented and reasonable partnership, he with his solo jobs and I with mine. But always with work and play together, conducted under a satisfactory system of dual control." Since she was insistent that both partners should contribute to the success of the relationship and held to that principle in finances as well, she demanded that they split household expenses. They lived for a time at the Wyndham Hotel on Fifty-eighth Street in New York and later relied on domestic help to keep up the Rye house and to deal with most of the cooking.

In December 1930 Amelia received a single lesson in an experimental aircraft called the Autogiro, a predecessor to the modern helicopter. The machine had been invented by the Spaniard Juan de la Cierva and was marketed by his American partner, Harold Pitcairn, who had begun Eastern Air Transport four years earlier and created the dependable Mailwing biplanes for delivering mail. The newly designed ship contained a normal-looking fuselage and a standard 300-horsepower Wright Whirlwind engine. Above the Autogiro's open cockpit, four long rotors, each with a diameter of forty-five feet, spun at one hundred revolutions per minute, allowing the craft to jump into the air from a standing position and then take flight. Amelia's instruction, given by Pitcairn's test pilot, James G. Ray, consisted of twenty minutes of flying around the Pitcairn company's Willow Grove, Pennsylvania, field and two landings. Ray told her to fly the craft and she took off, later admitting she didn't know "whether I flew it or it flew me."

Soon after they were married, Putnam ordered one for her. While waiting for her own Autogiro to arrive, she flew in another borrowed from the Pitcairn-Cierva Autogiro Company, and while trying to determine the ceiling for the gangly-looking craft, set an altitude record. She had arranged for a National Aeronautic Association sealed barograph to be installed before she made the attempt, and Putnam exhibited his keen publicity prowess by inviting Movietone News as well as reporters from New York and the wire services to witness the flight. On April 8 Amelia donned a heavy flying suit, boots, and mittens to protect her from cold temperatures aloft, and carried an oxygen bottle for help in breathing at high altitude, then took off and reached eighteen thousand feet. In a second flight, after most of the five hundred or so onlookers had left, she stayed aloft for about three hours and reached 18,415 feet, a new record for any person flying an Autogiro.

Following this exploit, Putnam made an arrangement with the Beech-Nut Packing Company, manufacturers of chewing gum and tinned food products, to buy the Autogiro and let Amelia fly the craft across the country. Company executives had already been intrigued by the advertising possibilities of the machine, and she wanted to become the first person to fly across the continent in it. In late April Amelia underwent surgery for a tonsillectomy and, still hoarse and weak, began her cross-country flight on May 29, departing from Newark with mechanic Eddie de Vaught accompanying her. Promoter Putnam handed out large packages of Beech-Nut gum, even enlisting the aid of his son David to boost the opening flight of the marketing tour. Meantime, G.P. had already added his name as a partner to the Brewer and Warren firm and one of the books he would soon publish was *Wings of Tomorrow* by inventor Juan de la Cierva, telling of the creation of the strange new ship.

The vivid green giro, described by the *Wyoming State Tribune* as a "weird windmill," needed to be fueled about every two hours, and Amelia often landed ten times during the day. Stopping in Cheyenne, Wyoming, on June 4, 1931, she planned further fueling stops at

Laramie, Parco, Rock Springs, and Leroy, Wyoming, before heading to Salt Lake City. As was typical of her stopovers, she drew enthusiastic crowds, and the *Tribune* estimated that half of the population of Cheyenne flocked to the airfield to see her. When she arrived in Oakland, California, on June 6, a throng of onlookers surged through the barricades to catch a glimpse of her. Only then did she discover that she had not been the first person to fly an Autogiro across the country. A pilot named Johnny Miller had completed that journey a couple of weeks before. To set a record, she needed to make a round-trip, and so set off toward the east. During her twenty-one-day tour, she flew an average speed of about eighty miles per hour, five hours daily, skipping only two days, and visiting seventy-six towns.

One of the Autogiro's selling points was its ease of flight. Amelia's trip west seemed to prove the claim; however, not all pilots agreed with the company's assessment and accidents were common. She crashed on June 12 in Abilene, Texas, when the wind stilled beneath the craft, eliminating any lift to the wings as she tried to take off and the Autogiro dropped thirty feet to the ground, damaging its rotor and propeller. Several cars parked nearby were struck by debris and the mob of people who had gathered close to watch might have been injured as well except that Amelia, aware of their presence, quickly aimed the faltering giro into an open space. The onlookers said a whirlwind had caused the crash; the Aeronautics Branch of the Department of

Commerce, the federal regulators of pilot safety, issued a formal reprimand, stating the accident was the result of pilot carelessness. Her pride was hurt but she was not banned from flying, although the Department of Commerce threatened to ground her for ninety days. However, Hiram Bingham, president of the N.A.A., interceded on her behalf and the penalty was not imposed.

Putnam booked her on two more Autogiro tours. In Detroit, Michigan, on September 12, during the Michigan State Fair, she pancaked when landing near the grandstand and then ground-looped after failing to level off properly before attempting to land. Putnam, who had traveled with her, drove to the fairgrounds and, while visiting with someone, heard the commotion and went running to rescue his wife, who was uninjured. In his urgency to reach her, he failed to see a guy wire, tripped on it, and fell hard, cracking three ribs and spraining his ankle. He was hospitalized briefly in Detroit.

Solo

Would you *mind* if I flew the Atlantic?" Amelia floated the question to her husband over breakfast at their Rye, New York, home one April morning in 1932.

Putnam realized the idea must have been on her mind for some time, probably since she had ridden as a passenger across the ocean four years before. During those years, she logged an additional thousand hours of flight time in the midst of her lectures and public appearances. She had been elected as the president of the Ninety-Nines, Inc., the previous September, heading the group that had grown to include 285 of the nation's 512 licensed women pilots, and continued to champion the efforts of women in aviation. The promotional possibilities of a solo transatlantic flight did not escape Putnam, yet now Amelia was his wife, and letting her go on such a hazardous jaunt, thrilling as it might be, felt frightening. Numerous persons attempting to cross the Atlantic since Lindbergh's successful solo flight in 1927 had perished in their attempts. Rye neighbor and fellow pilot Ruth Nichols had begun her own transatlantic quest in June 1931, only to suffer a nearly fatal crash in Saint John, New Brunswick, on the first leg of the flight. She had damaged five vertebrae in her back but despite the doubts of doctors, had begun flying again about a month after the accident, even setting a transcontinental women's speed record in October. Nichols was now preparing an attempt to fly the ocean again.

Putnam glanced across the newspaper at his wife awaiting his answer. He could not dash her dream, and the two decided to invite Bernt Balchen to lunch to ask his opinion. Balchen had flown Byrd across the Atlantic in 1927 and to the Antarctic in 1929, and they both trusted his judgment. As they played a game of croquet on the lawn, Amelia asked Balchen if he felt she was ready for such a flight, if her Vega could stand the journey, and if he thought she could succeed. He considered her questions, gave a positive answer to all of them, and even agreed to help her.

Amelia would charter her plane to Balchen, thus avoiding press attention while she completed preflight preparations. Observers would simply believe that the plane was being outfitted for Balchen's planned Antarctic expedition with explorer Lincoln Ellsworth. This allowed her the freedom to call off the flight for any reason without embarrassment and especially if Balchen, during their preparations, voiced doubts about her abilities or the airworthiness of the Vega. She was concerned that the press would get wind of the flight and wanted to avoid the additional pressure news coverage would place upon her. She later wrote, "I wanted to fly because I *wanted* to; not because advance publicity compelled me to." Also, by keeping silent about her plans, she reduced the possibility that other competitors—like Ruth Nichols—would try to beat her to the punch.

Amelia had been writing a book, *The Fun of It*, to promote women and their aviation achievements, and wanted to make this trip for the sheer pleasure of doing it. A woman who delighted in *"first-time* things," she wanted to be the first woman to solo the Atlantic. But there was another, more deep-seated motive. She felt that all the accolades heaped upon her following the successful crossing of the *Friendship* were undeserved; that those laurels were more publicity-based than founded upon her skill. She had wanted to pilot the *Friendship* at least part of the way but had only taken the controls between Burry Port and Southampton. Now she wanted to prove her worth as a pilot, most of all to herself, and to make the commendations ring true.

She could not contain her excitement over the upcoming flight and revealed her plan to her cousin, Lucy Challis, who was staying with her in Rye, but swore Challis to secrecy. The only other person who would learn of the flight prior to takeoff was her mechanic

Eddie Gorski, Bernt Balchen's assistant and a former mechanic for the Fokker aircraft company.

During April and into May 1932, Amelia worked on improving her instrument skills and learning to fly "blind." She pored over meteorological charts and maps with Dr. James "Doc" Kimball of the United States Weather Bureau in New York, well respected among pilots for his weather-predicting skill. He had been celebrated by transatlantic fliers the previous year, and she had featured the weatherman in one of her *Cosmopolitan* columns. She needed to learn as much as she could from Kimball about what weather she could expect during her flight in order to calculate the fuel load. How strong would the headwinds be? Where were storms forming? What weather patterns usually existed over the North Atlantic? These matters were crucial to a successful flight.

While she educated herself on the weather, Balchen and Gorski prepared the Vega by strengthening the wooden fuselage. This reinforcement was required to hold the 420 gallons of fuel and 20 gallons of oil that would sustain the new, supercharged Pratt and Whitney 500-horsepower Wasp engine through thirty-two hundred miles of flight. As well, they installed additional instruments to aid the pilot, including a drift indicator, a magnetic compass, an aperiodic compass that had a more stable needle than the magnetic compass, and a Sperry directional gyro, which was not affected by magnetism, for extra navigational security. (Army Major Edwin

Aldrin, later father of the astronaut "Buzz" Aldrin, a crewman on the second Apollo space flight to the moon, supervised the fueling for the monoplane.)

By mid-May, with the weather remaining uncooperative, Amelia drove to the Teterboro, New Jersey, airport daily to fly. On May 18 weather maps indicated a low-pressure area in the eastern Atlantic that was likely to remain in position for several days. The next morning she expected only to fly practice runs when a call from her husband alerted her to Doc Kimball's assessment that a window of opportunity existed over the ocean and that the weather to Harbor Grace, Newfoundland, was clear. After a quick discussion with Balchen, they set the departure time for 3:00 P.M.

She rushed back to Rye, told the cook not to expect her for dinner, donned clean flying togs—jodhpurs, silk shirt, scarf, and windbreaker—grabbed her flying suit, a toothbrush, and a comb and prepared rations consisting of canned tomato juice and a thermos of chicken soup. She then raced back to the airport, arriving five minutes before three o'clock. Within twenty minutes, with Balchen piloting the fifty-five-hundred-pound Vega and Gorski and Amelia riding in the fuselage behind the extra fuel tank, they took off. She had napped during the three-hour-and-thirty-minute trip to St. John, New Brunswick. They spent the night there, then flew to Harbor Grace, Newfoundland, the next day. Then she rested again in preparation for the long flight ahead, waiting for the fog to dissipate.

Balchen recalled her arrival at the Canadian airfield after he had called to give her the go-ahead and as he instructed her about the flight plan he had prepared. She listened carefully as he told her about the course to take and about the weather to expect during her flight. He wrote, "She looks at me with a small lonely smile and says, 'Do you think I can make it?' and I grin back: 'You bet.'"

Before she departed that Friday evening, she said a few words, exuding confidence, to the gathered group of local and United States reporters: "To all my friends, both far and near, let me say that you will hear from me in less than fifteen hours." Balchen, she recalled, said to her, "Okeh. So-long. Good luck." She climbed into the cockpit, revved the engine, checked the magnetos, and gave a go-ahead nod. When Gorski and Balchen removed the chocks, she taxied to starting position, then sped away, coaxing her heavy ship into the air at 7:12 P.M.

The New York Times on May 20, 1932, carried some words from Balchen on the hazards of her flight: "Mrs. Putnam has ninety-nine chances out of a hundred to cross the Atlantic if she gets an even break." He added a remark that bespoke his belief in her abilities—"She is probably the greatest woman pilot of today."

About four hours into the flight, Amelia encountered the storms and the instrument malfunctions that threatened to destroy her dream and, worse, to take her life. Relying on her pilot training, she kept calm and persevered throughout the long, lonely night, coping as best she could despite the broken altimeter, a malfunctioning tachometer, and the dangers of the icy heights and ocean surface she flew between. The bright light of morning dimmed her view of the persistent flames eating through the collector ring of the exhaust manifold, and although she knew from her experience with engines that the manifold often heated to a glowing red under normal use, this unexpected development had been different, and the resultant steady vibration had been annoying and tiresome. She opened the tomato juice can with an ice pick, and sipped it, hoping to quell the tightness in her belly that plagued her during all long-distance flights. Her queasy stomach and the possibility of becoming airsick precluded eating, and she was careful not to drink too much since the relief tubes provided for men to relieve their bladders did not work for women. She discovered, too, that during the night her reserve fuel tank had developed a leak, the bitter gasoline fumes now burning her eyes and making her head ache even more as she squinted against the brilliance of the sun's reflection off the white clouds. She descended to a place within the clouds to rest her eyes, took a whiff of smelling salts, and began searching for land.

Beneath the clouds she saw a fishing boat, then several more. She deviated from her set compass course, flying northeast, thinking that due to the northwest direction of the winds she had drifted south of her route. She saw a coastline—Ireland—then, when a railroad track came into view, she followed it, certain that it would lead to an airfield. She didn't find one, so she searched for any good landing spot, coming down in a verdant pasture and scattering a herd of cows.

She landed close to a cottage, not by design but because she didn't see it until she was almost upon it. Her eyes were strained and tired from the lengthy flight and the bright sunlight in her face. She looked at the cockpit clock, and discovered her trip had been completed in fourteen hours and fifty-six minutes.

Dan McCallion, a cow herder, ran toward her. "Have you come far?"

"I've come from America," she told him.

He later recalled he was "all stunned and didn't know what to say."

She had landed on the William Gallegher farm, and after the owners gave her a drink of water and some tea, Gallegher drove her to Londonderry, about five miles away, to telephone her husband. Since the Galleghers invited her to stay the night with them, she returned to the farm to make sure her plane was guarded against souvenir hunters and curious onlookers, then returned to Londonderry to place five more three-minute calls to G.P. This time, a crowd gathered and kept Amelia busy until 10:00 P.M., when she finally went to bed.

Putnam had been waiting all night, tense and pacing, although he had publicly stated his "complete confidence" in his wife. A report that Amelia's plane had crashed in Paris nearly undid him, but when her jubilant call came twelve minutes later, he finally relaxed. His triumphant wife had not only achieved her dream of conquering the Atlantic, but had become the only person to fly across the ocean twice and broke the record for the fastest crossing in any direction. She also broke Ruth Nichols's record for the longest nonstop distance flown by a woman, logging 2,026 miles.

On Sunday morning a refreshed Amelia faced the press and confronted the piles of correspondence that had begun to arrive. The first congratulatory note came from the Lindberghs who were suffering devastating grief over the kidnapping and murder of their son about a week before Amelia's flight. Their excitement at her achievement was recorded in Anne Morrow Lindbergh's diary on May 21, 1932: "Amelia landed in Ireland!"

Lady Astor, the former Nancy Langhorne of Virginia, the first female member of Parliament, sent word that she would lend Amelia a nightgown; her mother and sister sent a message displaying their pride in and love for her; and a representative of King George V expressed the pleasure of the royal family in her accomplishment. President Herbert Hoover wrote, "I voice the pride of the nation in congratulating you most heartily upon achieving the splendid pioneer solo flight by a woman across the Atlantic Ocean. You have demonstrated not only your own dauntless courage but also the capacity of women to match the skill of men in carrying through the most difficult feats of high adventure."

A Paramount News plane took her to London where

she disembarked during a rainstorm. As she began to make a speech to the throng awaiting her arrival, a thunderclap interrupted; she laughed, and the crowd adored her unassuming manner. In London she stayed with Andrew W. Mellon, the United States ambassador to England, and borrowed a dress, coat, hat, gloves, and shoes from his daughter. As she had told reporters, "The only clothing I have with me is my flying suit on my back and the only money I have is $20 that was handed to me as I was leaving. I haven't even a check to sign." G.P. had given her the money; she later signed the twenty-dollar bill and gave it back to him as a memento.

Since Hilton Railey was not present to handle the press and arrange for the correspondence to be answered, Putnam had contacted one of his agents in London to help with the reporters, but Amelia had to answer the stacks of telegrams commending her for the flight. There were also rounds of teas and celebrations and luncheons and press conferences. She toasted King George V with water, making headlines because she did not drink alcohol, and later donned a green satin gown and danced with the Prince of Wales (the future Edward VIII) until the orchestra retired. Selfridge's department store put her Vega on display, and Amelia, as was customary with celebrities of the day, "signed" her name in the glass window with a special diamond-point pen.

She had not thought it necessary for G.P. to join her immediately, but after the first two days, changed her mind. He was attending an important business meeting in California, one that ultimately resulted in his becoming the chief of the Paramount Studios editorial board, but broke away and made the voyage to England aboard the *Olympia*. Meantime, Amelia continued her schedule of public appearances, explaining that she had made the flight for the pure pleasure of it and predicting that transatlantic air travel would one day become routine.

Putnam arrived in Cherbourg, France, on June 3 and Amelia traveled aboard a private yacht to meet him. They moved on together to Paris, where, at the Hotel Lotti, a mob of well-wishers shouted greetings until she waved at them from the balcony. She was the first woman presented to the French Senate and there received the Knight's Cross of the Legion of Honor; she attended air races and laid a wreath at the tomb of the unknown soldier; and in Rome, she and Putnam met privately with the pope and the Italian dictator, Benito Mussolini. They attended the Congress of Trans-Oceanic Airmen in Rome, with Amelia the only female among the highly decorated fliers. (While the Italians did not present her with a decoration, apparently believing such privileges to be reserved for men, several years later, they relented and sent her a medal. She also received the Order of Virtutea Aviation from Rumania, additional honors from the French and Belgian Aero Clubs, and recognition from numerous cities and groups in the United States.) The Putnams then journeyed to Brussels and enjoyed a private luncheon with King Albert and Queen Elisabeth of Belgium, who bestowed upon the victorious pilot that country's Chevalier of the Order of Leopold.

On June 15 the Putnams boarded the *Île de France* to return to the United States, and three light airplanes flew over the ship, dropping bouquets in her honor. The journey home gave her a chance to rest, to prepare for the festivities awaiting her, and to catch up with G.P. and discuss the numerous public appearances and endorsements he had scheduled on her behalf.

When the liner reached New York, all the seafaring vessels in the harbor serenaded her with their whistles, and adding to the racket, nine Army planes, three Douglas observation planes, and three Navy Curtiss Fledglings flew overhead. She boarded the *Riverside,* the welcoming boat provided by the city, and discovered among those greeting her were her stepson, David Putnam, and friends Eugene Vidal and Paul Collins from the Ludington Line, Bernt Balchen, and Amy Phipps Guest, who had initiated the *Friendship* flight five years before. Her mother and sister did not join her in the New York festivities. Putnam had written to Amy Earhart before he sailed to Europe and invited them to make arrangements with Hilton Railey if they wished to join in the welcome, but he also suggested that they could visit him and Amelia later in Rye when things had quieted down.

On board the *Riverside,* Amelia met with the press, posed for photographers, and invited the female pilots who had come to greet her to be included. On shore, she rode in a car with Charles L. Lawrance, designer of the Kinner Airster engine and now the president of the Aeronautical Chamber of Commerce, enjoying the confetti-throwing and cheering of a ticker-tape parade. Following the parade, she attended a luncheon held in her honor at the Waldorf-Astoria, and afterward, at a separate event, received the first gold medal presented by the Society of Woman Geographers.

The next day, she flew to Washington, D.C., aboard a Ludington Line trimotor, accompanied by G.P. and David, her cousin Lucy Challis, Paul Collins of the airline, and Bernt Balchen. In the capital, she was to be awarded the National Geographic Society's medal, and the group's president, Gilbert Grosvenor, met her at the airport and escorted her to the White House where newsreel cameras had been set up to record her meeting with President Hoover. Grosvenor hosted her at lunch, then introduced her to numerous governmental dignitaries and accompanied her to the House of Representatives and the Senate, the members of which had decided to award her the Distinguished Flying Cross, with the presentation to be made at a later date. That evening, wearing a pale blue crepe gown, she again visited the White House, this time for a formal dinner, after which the entourage went to Constitution Hall for the formal presentation of the Geographic Society medal. She became the first woman to receive the honor, and President Hoover made the presentation before a crowd of thirty-eight hundred people. (Ten thousand had applied for tickets.) He said, "Her accomplishments combine to place her in spirit with the great pioneering women to whom every generation of Americans has looked up with admiration for their firmness of will, their strength of character, and their cheerful spirit of comradeship in the work of the world."

In her acceptance speech, broadcast over the NBC radio network, she said she considered the honors bestowed on her "out of proportion to the deed itself," and further explained she would be pleased "if my small exploit has drawn attention to the fact that women, too, are flying."

Bearings

ollowing her appearance in Washington, Amelia, as she had done four years before, toured the country for her adoring public and to promote her book, *The Fun of It,* which G.P. astutely released the week she returned from Europe. Each first edition contained inside the front cover a small phonograph record of her broadcast message from London. Her schedule included a day in Boston, where she visited with her mother, Amy, and sister, Muriel Morrissey, at Muriel's home in Medford before returning to New York to meet other commitments.

Her relationship with Amy and Muriel had struck some rocky ground after her marriage to Putnam. Her mother had not approved of G.P. and apparently didn't change her opinion after they were wed. She did not come to visit the couple in Rye even though she'd been

invited. Correspondence also shows Amelia's exaspera-
tion with her family over money matters. Specifically,
she sent monthly support checks to her mother and
voiced her irritation when she believed Amy shared
some of those funds with the Morrisseys. She even
threatened to withhold some of the money if her
mother didn't follow her instructions and use the funds
for herself.

Despite their differences, Amelia wrote often to Amy
and continued to try to look after her. Her mother was
living with the Morrisseys and helping keep the house
and watch the children, another matter that annoyed
Amelia, who did not think her mother needed to be
doing such menial chores. She had earlier been an-
gered because the Morrisseys failed to prepare a loan
document for her after she lent them $2,500 for the
mortgage on their house, and twice asked that such
paperwork acknowledging her investment be given to
her. She had also offered advice to Muriel, who was
enduring difficulties in her marriage following the birth
of her second child, about seeking medical advice for
birth-control methods and suggesting that Muriel's
husband should share in that responsibility.

In July 1932 Amelia flew G.P. and David to Los Angeles on business and a few days later announced that
she would try to set a record on her trip back to Newark,
New Jersey. She wanted to beat barnstormer Frank
Hawks's transcontinental speed record and to best the
women's time set by her Rye neighbor, Ruth Nichols.

A faulty gas line in the Vega forced an unexpected landing in Columbus, Ohio, ruining Amelia's chances of beating Hawks's time, but she continued on with the flight, shaving ten hours from Nichols's elapsed time despite the delay.

She returned to Los Angeles to see the Olympic Games with G.P. and David and two days before the opening ceremonies, Vice President Charles Curtis awarded her the Distinguished Flying Cross for "displaying heroic courage and skill as a navigator at the risk of her life" during her transatlantic solo. (The Seventy-second Congress had voted to award her the prestigious medal following the flight.) She wrote in the August 1932 issue of *American Magazine,* "My particular inner desire to fly the Atlantic alone was nothing new with me. I had flown Atlantics before. Everyone has his own Atlantics to fly. Whatever you want very much to do, against the opposition of tradition, neighborhood opinion, and so-called 'common sense'—that is an Atlantic."

Although she spent some time with her family, especially enjoying riding and swimming with her stepsons, she continued to sharpen her flight skills. She again attempted to best Hawks's time on August 25, 1932, and broke the cross-country distance record of 2,478 miles while beating her own previous speed by almost ten minutes. She became the first woman to fly nonstop coast to coast but Hawks's record stood.

That fall, she pressed President Hoover to support passage of an equal rights amendment for women. She had joined the National Women's Party and believed wholeheartedly that women who performed similar work to that of men deserved to receive wages equal to those of their counterparts.

Early in the new year, the Putnams hosted a dinner party at their Rye home, mainly so G.P. could entice Belgian balloonist Auguste Piccard to write a book about his adventures. Charles and Anne Lindbergh and several others also attended. During the evening, Piccard enthralled everyone with his knowledge of aviation and spoke of his high-altitude adventures. The conversation, complete with quotes from Lindy, appeared in the next issue of *The New York Times*. The story created friction between G.P. and the Lindberghs, who had thought they were attending a private dinner. The matter was settled after Piccard's business manager admitted he had sold the story to the press for forty dollars.

In late January Amelia toured the West, speaking briefly in Helena, Montana, to state legislators, and presenting her usual lectures in Oregon, Washington, and British Columbia. A Spokane reporter described her courteous manner with those who greeted her at the hotel, calling her "a lovely feminine-looking young woman" and admiring her full-length fur coat and the bouquet of pink sweet peas she carried with her. At the end of her tour, she lunched in Los Angeles with G.P., who had been commuting for his work for Paramount Studios. Her appearance sparked rumors that she would soon serve as an aviation consultant for the movies, and later in the year, *Screenland* magazine ran a feature on Amelia containing a photograph of her with movie star Gary Cooper who was portraying a pilot in a forthcoming film.

In March 1933 Amelia and her husband attended, at Eleanor Roosevelt's invitation, the inauguration of President Franklin D. Roosevelt and on April 20 they returned to the White House for a dinner and an overnight stay. On this night, after the meal and dressed in formal evening gown and white gloves, she called Eastern Air Transport to arrange for a plane and pilots, and took Mrs. Roosevelt on a round-trip flight from Washington to Baltimore. A number of women reporters were invited to ride along, as well as G.P., the First Lady's brother, Hall Roosevelt, and Eugene Vidal.

Amelia did not fly the plane but took the controls long enough for photographs to be taken, and Mrs. Roosevelt did as well. One image of the event shows a smiling, white-gloved Amelia, her tousled hair in its usual disarray, pointing out landmarks through the window to the beaming, feather-hatted first lady. Eleanor so enjoyed her night flight that Amelia helped her arrange for the physical examination required of pilots, and Mrs. Roosevelt obtained her student permit. The president, however, squelched her plans for taking flight lessons.

On the day after their flight, Amelia spoke to the Daughters of the American Revolution at Constitution

Hall, chiding the members for their support of a re-armament bill in Congress. She believed that the D.A.R. should not back such legislation unless the women were willing to serve in the military themselves, and her speech drew some criticism. She sometimes aired her pacifist views during her lecture tours but seldom received rebukes.

She stood on her principles in other matters as well. When the National Aeronautic Association decided to allow its in-house magazine to be produced by independent contractors to improve profits, Amelia, serving as vice president and the first woman officer of the organization, protested publicly. Hiram Bingham, the group's president, took umbrage at her action but the two had already had differences of opinion over other issues and much negative publicity and stern correspondence between them ensued. Bingham thought that Amelia's stand was actually a ploy to support her husband's plan to start a new magazine himself. She soon resigned from the vice presidency.

That summer she teamed with former airline colleagues Paul Collins and Eugene Vidal and Washington-based real-estate magnate Sam Solomon to form another company in conjunction with the Boston and Maine Railroad. National Airways, most often referred to as Boston and Maine Airways, was to begin operations in early August, serving the towns of Portland, Rockland, Bangor, and Augusta. Each of the partners contributed $2,500 to the new company's capital.

In June 1933 Amelia and Ruth Nichols were invited to participate in the Bendix Race, the all-male bastion of air racing named for industrialist Vincent Bendix, and the opening event of the National Air Races. The two women pilots received only two weeks' notice that they could compete but a special $2,000 prize was offered to the fastest female flier as compensation for the late notification of their eligibility. In addition, race officials allowed the women a six-hour handicap.

Amelia had sold her historic red Vega to the Franklin Institute in January for $7,500 and saw the race as a sterling opportunity to try out her new Vega "High Speed Special," equipped with a larger fin and rudder and a 700-horsepower Wasp motor. The plane had been owned previously by Elinor Smith, the pilot who had flown beneath New York City's bridges. Nichols, who had crashed her Lockheed Vega during her transatlantic flight attempt, spent a full week arranging for the loan of another airplane, a low-winged, long-nosed 550-horsepower Lockheed Orion. A further delay ensued when her mechanic decided he needed test pilot Wiley Post's help in tuning the engine. Post, however, had just embarked on an around-the-world flight.

Both women were beset by difficulties during the competition. Amelia was forced down in Wichita after strong headwinds caused her motor to overheat. The next day she made a forced landing in Winslow, Arizona, because, according to *The New York Times,* the hatch cover on her Vega "blew off and 'blanketed' the tail,

making it extremely difficult to control." She arrived at
Mines Field in Los Angeles later that day while another
race was in progress and had to circle the field above the
forty-eight thousand spectators for thirty minutes until
the competition was completed. Colonel Roscoe Turner
of New York won the Bendix in a Weddell-Williams
racer with a Wasp engine, breaking his own transcontinental speed record with an elapsed time of eleven hours
and thirty minutes and earning an additional $1,000
bonus for the swift time. *The Times* reported that Amelia
called Putnam after landing, and "told him that the flight
she had just completed was the most hazardous of the
eighteen transcontinental hops she has made and 'four
times as dangerous' as her Atlantic flight."

Nichols suffered her own troubles, and following a
battle with a drooping landing gear that required tiresome hand-pumping to retract, she also had to land in
Wichita. She again had trouble after leaving Albuquerque, and had to return there, arriving at Mines
Field on July 3.

On that same day, *The Times* carried an article quot-
ing Putnam as reporting Amelia wanted to try to break
her transcontinental nonstop speed record. On July 9
she did so, but not without surmounting dangerous ob-
stacles. When the hatch cover worked loose again, she
held it in her right hand for seventy-five miles until she
could land in Amarillo, Texas. She stopped a second
time to refuel in Columbus, Ohio, and arrived in
Newark that evening.

Later that month, record-setting English fliers James and Amy Mollison, with whom Amelia had become acquainted following her transatlantic solo, took off from London headed to Newfoundland with the intention of landing at Roosevelt Field in New York. The westbound ocean crossing was James Mollison's second. He had soloed the route before. Amelia and G.P. were staying with friends in Purchase, New York, and listened to radio reports of the flight. When the startling news was broadcast that Mollison had missed landing at Roosevelt and while attempting to set down at Bridgeport, Connecticut, overshot the runway and crashed, Amelia took action. She visited the Mollisons in the hospital and invited them to stay in Rye to recuperate from their injuries. They informally created a new club for the few pilots still living who had successfully crossed the North Atlantic by plane. In addition to Amelia and James Mollison, the only others eligible were Charles Lindbergh, Wiley Post, and James Mattern. The next weekend, President Roosevelt invited the Putnams and the Mollisons to lunch with him at Hyde Park.

Putnam landed a deal in 1934 that made Amelia into a dress designer modeling her own line of classic, comfortable clothes for active women, and receiving good initial response. She had earlier spoken with designer Elsa Schiaparelli in Rye about creating better outfits for women, including longer shirttails so that the wearer could stretch and bend without worrying about revealing her midriff, and making waistlines in dresses conform to a woman's body rather than to an industry standard. Amelia suggested that parachute silk be used to make shirts and that other details—such as buttons made to resemble oil cups, and wrinkle-resistant, washable fabrics with designs resembling nuts and bolts and other similar devices—be inspired by aviation. Amelia also suggested jackets and skirts be marketed separately rather than as suits so that women could purchase items tailored to their figures, a new development in apparel merchandising. The line premiered at Macy's department store in New York, and Putnam contracted with several New York firms for the manufacturing, including the John B. Stetson Company, which produced the matching hats.

Although she had completed her term as president of the Ninety-Nines, she gave the women pilots an incentive to log more flight hours throughout the country, offering one of her specially designed Stetsons to the pilot who flew to the most airports each month.

She worked on designs with a seamstress in her apartment at the Hotel Seymour in between her public appearances. Putnam's business acumen expanded beyond clothing and had included deals for Amelia to tout spark plugs, airplane and vehicle oils, and cameras. Consumers could also purchase Amelia Earhart Time-Savers stationery and Amelia Earhart luggage.

From the beginning, since her selection as the woman to ride on the *Friendship,* Amelia had been considered the female Lindbergh. She now had flown the Atlantic as he had—alone—which seemed to make the nickname "Lady Lindy" even more appropriate. The comparison, however, bothered her, so much so that following her solo, she had written an apology to Anne Lindbergh. The Lindberghs took the matter lightly; they had been among the first to congratulate her on her successful ocean crossing both times and sent another laudatory telegram after receiving news of her record-breaking transcontinental flight.

The transatlantic solo had strengthened Amelia's confidence, allowing her at last to stand beyond the shadow of the mighty Minnesotan, Lindy, but she longed to make another long-distance flight, one that would prove her skill as a pilot, satisfy her yearning for "first-time things," and thus, by association, elevate the future of women in aviation.

Turbulence

I n July 1934 Amelia and G.P. traveled to Wyoming for a two-week vacation, their first true getaway together since their wedding. They stayed at the Double Dee Ranch owned by Putnam's friend, Carl Dunrud, the rancher who had accompanied him on his journeys to Greenland and Baffin Island in 1926 and 1927. They camped, fly-fished, hiked, and rode horses, and Dunrud gave Amelia's brunette locks a trim. She later wrote in *Outdoors* magazine that her pilot skills far exceeded her fishing abilities, but the ranch near Mee-teetse, Wyoming, charmed her. She planned to come back and made plans with Putnam to have a log cabin built near the deserted mining town of Kirwin, not far from Dunrud's ranch.

After returning to Rye, New York, that fall, she casually announced to her husband that she'd like to fly across the Pacific Ocean. Soon after that they rented a house in Toluca Lake, California, another place Amelia loved, near Paul Mantz, a Hollywood stunt pilot and charter service owner, so Mantz could provide expert technical advice for Amelia's proposed flight and overhaul her Vega at the United Airport. The press, in early October, picked up rumors that she was planning another long-distance flight, either from Natal, Brazil, across the southern Atlantic to Africa, or from San Francisco to Honolulu, but she denied these stories. She actually had planned a flight from Honolulu to California, since no pilot had soloed that part of the ocean from west to east, reasoning that she could more easily find the California coastline from the air than small islands in the sea. Putnam, meantime, had remained in New York and in late November called her with the sad news that a fire had partially destroyed their Rye home. Among the treasured items lost was a trunk storing Amelia's papers, including her poems and childhood papers, and letters. G.P., who mourned the loss of his collection of Rockwell Kent paintings, set about rebuilding. He joined his wife on the West Coast in mid-December.

The two boarded the *Lurline* on December 22, 1934, bound for the Hawaiian Islands. Amelia told reporters they were going for a vacation with friends Paul Mantz, his wife, Myrtle, and his mechanic, Ernie Tissot. However, Mantz had served as her technical adviser for some time and her scarlet Vega, trimmed with sporty gold stripes, stood conspicuously strapped to the aft deck on the tennis court of the *Lurline*. When journalists pressed her about bringing her airplane along, she said she might take some flights over the islands. In mid-ocean, she and Mantz tried out the new radio equipment he had installed in the Vega, reaching Kingman, Arizona, at least a thousand miles away from the liner, and tested the rebuilt motor several times to prevent corrosion from the salty sea air. They spent Christmas on board ship, and Amelia wrote to her mother the next day, revealing her flight plan. If her idea worked out, she would fly from Honolulu to Oakland and then on to Washington.

After arriving in Honolulu on December 27, Amelia and her husband stayed on Waikiki Beach at the home of Chris Holmes, Putnam's millionaire friend. She basked in the sun on the lanai, rode outrigger canoes, and took leisurely walks on the beach, breathing in the briny scent of the ocean. She gave one lecture, "Flying for Fun," at the University of Hawaii.

But relaxing on the beach, welcome respite that it was, served only as a soothing backdrop for her plan to fly from Hawaii to California and then perhaps continue on to Washington as she had discussed with G.P. that fall. Although no one person had flown that ocean route, it had been crossed by aircraft several times in the past, most recently by renowned Australian aviator Charles Kingsford-Smith and his navigator.

As she worked with Mantz and mechanic Tissot to

prepare for flight, controversy erupted over a publicity deal Putnam made with certain Hawaiian businessmen. Amelia was to receive $10,000 from a group of Hawaiian sugar growers to promote the islands by mentioning them in her articles and publicity tours when she returned to the States. An article in the magazine *Editor and Publisher* called the flight a publicity stunt sponsored by the Pan Pacific Press Bureau, an advertising organization representing Hawaiian sugar growers, which had mistakenly sent a confidential memo to the magazine. Further, rumors about the proposed flight were started and then denied, a ploy, critics said, to give the event even more attention. The idea backfired and Putnam denied he had organized the plan, but more criticism was leveled by the *San Francisco News* and the *Honolulu Star-Bulletin,* which asserted that the sugar growers resented a tariff on products exported to the States. If they could convince powerful government officials that Hawaii was "an integral part of the United States," something that Amelia could draw attention to as a result of her flight, the tax requirement might be lifted and parity with mainland sugar producers could be achieved.

Additional criticism surfaced about the flight itself. If something were to go wrong, Navy personnel would have to risk their lives to search for and rescue her, and the taxpayers would foot the bill for an estimated million dollars. The potential for an expensive and nerve-racking search had been thrown into focus in early

December when Lieutenant Charles T. P. Ulm, a crew member of Kingsford-Smith's 1928 Pacific flight on the trimotor *Southern Cross,* had attempted to fly from California to Australia. He took off from Oakland bound for Honolulu—and vanished. In contrast, Amelia's Vega was equipped with a single engine and to make the flight would be loaded with 520 gallons of fuel and 35 gallons of oil. Hers would be the first civilian long-distance flight to use a two-way radio phone, allowing her to contact radio stations on land as she flew. The equipment itself, weighing eighty pounds, sat behind the cockpit, but Amelia would have easy access to the microphone and the volume and selector switches. She had to roll out the antenna, knobbed with a small steel ball, through a hole in the floor by using a reel beneath her seat, and then retract it for takeoffs and landings.

The *Honolulu Star-Bulletin* suggested in an editorial that Amelia should avoid putting lives unnecessarily at risk and the United States Navy entered the fray, airing concerns that her radio equipment did not have sufficient range needed for the long-distance flight. Then, Mantz flew the plane to twelve thousand feet and contacted Kingman, Arizona, squelching these worries.

She did not reveal the tension created by the stinging comments, focusing instead on preflight preparations, part of which had included Mantz's instructions on how to make an emergency landing in the ocean without flipping the plane over. Other preparations included test flights to ensure proper venting of the gas tanks—letting air into the tanks as the fuel is consumed—and runs to calculate fuel consumption at a set rate of speed, as well as experiments to find the best setting for the Hamilton controllable pitch propeller. Mantz had removed the six passenger seats and replaced them with the nine fuel tanks she needed for the twenty-four-hundred-mile flight. She wrote a note to the military base commander at Wheeler Field in Honolulu, explaining she would not hold the military responsible if anything happened to her, and wrote to G.P., confiding that the flight had been made more difficult because of the "barrage of belittlement." She told him, "If I do not do a good job it will not be because the plane and motor are not excellent nor because women cannot fly."

The financial backers of the flight, made anxious by the negative preflight publicity, wanted to renege on their deal, and four days before her planned departure called a meeting and requested she cancel the flight. However, Amelia, who had already spent half of the money on preparations, stood her ground. She would fly whether or not they paid her the money. The businessmen followed the original agreement.

She planned to make a practice takeoff on January 11, 1935, and on that day, the islands were lashed by a heavy late-morning rain. Amelia rested at the Chris Holmes residence until noon, then went with Putnam to the home of Lieutenant George Sparhawk, a naval radio expert, for lunch. Mantz and naval weatherman Lieutenant E. W. Stephens joined them there. Putnam,

Mantz, and Stephens drove to Wheeler Field after lunch while Amelia napped until Lieutenant Sparhawk drove her to the airfield after the rain subsided. She arrived at about four-thirty.

Conditions there were daunting. The runway was not hard-surfaced, and the rain had rendered the airstrip, six thousand feet long and lined with small white flags, into a muddy path, increasing the hazards of takeoff in a nearly three-ton, fuel-laden airplane. A somber group of almost two hundred people, mostly military personnel and their families, gathered to watch. Three fire engines and an ambulance stood nearby.

While the weather in the islands was not favorable for flight, ocean conditions were good although expected to deteriorate. She had to chance a takeoff now or face a delay of unknown length. Putnam likely had something to say in the departure date as well—it coincided with the first anniversary of the flight of six Navy planes from San Francisco to Pearl Harbor, Hawaii, and it was a Friday, which meant that Amelia, were she successful, would be featured in the Sunday newspapers, gaining more publicity than she would on a weekday. The trial of Bruno Richard Hauptmann for the kidnapping and murder of Charles and Anne Lindbergh's baby had begun and space for other news was limited.

Amelia told reporters, "Sixty percent of the success of any expedition lies in its preparation, and I feel that I am prepared. I certainly anticipate no trouble." She climbed into the cockpit, wearing her brown fur-lined flying suit—incongruous clothing in the tropical heat of the islands but necessary for the high-altitude chill that would permeate the cabin once pilot and plane soared aloft. Putnam stuck his head inside the cockpit for a private farewell; she closed the isinglass cockpit cover, and he climbed down.

She nodded, the ground crew removed the chocks, and she gunned the supercharged Pratt and Whitney Wasp S1D1 engine, spurring the cumbersome fifty-eight-hundred-pound Vega down the mucky airstrip at 4:45 P.M. Mechanic Tissot ran alongside, mud sloshing around his shoes, a forlorn look on his pale face and cigarette drooping from his mouth, as if his movement and encouragement could help lift the airplane into the air. Amelia passed the halfway point—the point where she must turn back or go forward and face the consequences—and the Vega's tail rose. She hit a bump, the wind lifted her wings, she opened the throttle to full and the extra power helped NR 965 Y skyward. Not long after, she flew past the stately landmark of Diamond Head and soared above the vast turquoise sea, climbing to six thousand feet and switching her propeller into high gear to help increase her speed to an average of 150 miles per hour, the optimum for the timely consumption of her fuel load.

She wore an inflatable vest over her flying suit, carried a hatchet and a sheathed knife, and brought along an inflatable rubber raft with a sealed compartment filled with tomato juice, chocolate, malted milk tablets, and water, all stored behind the gas tanks. The two largest tanks contained dump valves that would allow her to dispose of the fuel if she had to make a forced landing. In the event of an ocean landing, the plane would likely nose beneath the surface, leaving the lighter tail end to linger above the waves long enough for Amelia to cut through the fabric-covered wood of the fuselage with her hatchet and retrieve the raft. She had a Very pistol to shoot red and green flares into the air and balloons to be raised on fish line tied with red flags to help signal her position to rescuers should she be forced to ditch. She had stocked her tiny larder with a thermos of hot chocolate, bottles of water, and a picnic lunch prepared for her by Lieutenant Sparhawk's wife, in addition to the extra portions of the foods carried in the life raft. In the small space in the wing near her shoulder, she stored her maps, which included a chart listing all the ships at sea, their locations, and the times she should fly over them, calculated on a certain starting time and average flying speed. Retired naval officer Clarence Williams had prepared her navigational maps, and she needed to check her bearings each hour during the flight to stay on course. Three clocks, two showing Honolulu and San Francisco time and one to indicate the elapsed time of her flight, also had been installed in the cockpit.

Local radio stations in Honolulu and California tracked her progress, and she listened to musical programs on the radio while she flew. She saw a ship and radioed, soon hearing about herself on her cockpit radio. In one communication, a Honolulu station patched through G.P., who asked her to talk louder into the microphone because engine noise was drowning her words. Static and atmospheric conditions also made it difficult for radio operators and station listeners to hear her entire transmissions. She made radio calls every half hour.

Three hours after takeoff she reported the temperature in the cockpit at forty-five degrees Fahrenheit. Just before midnight, she spotted a ship, the Matson liner *Maliko*. She could not communicate with the ship via her radio but blinked her landing lights, located on the leading edges of her wings, and soon heard on her radio that she had been sighted and learned of the ship's location, about nine hundred miles from the islands. During the night, the stars enchanted her, seeming "to rise from the sea and hang outside my cockpit window, near enough to touch." She enjoyed "the most memorable cup of hot chocolate I have ever had" and later drank some tomato juice and ate a hard-boiled egg.

Fog bedeviled her on the flight as it had in her previous ocean journeys, cloaking the water below. In one radio message, she reported she had tired of the fog, but those listening on the ground interpreted her comment as she had simply grown tired. She flew much of the way at about eight thousand feet, listening to musical programs on the radio, and picking up a performance by the San Francisco Symphony Orchestra in the early morning. The only uncomfortable part of the flight occurred when a ventilation cover blew off causing an intense stream of air to blow directly into her eye, making it sore and watery. There was no remedy; she had to withstand the irritation until she landed.

Still struggling with the misty conditions after fifteen hours of flight, a break in the clouds appeared and she glimpsed a ship below. She radioed to ask the vessel's identity, found it was the liner *President Pierce*, almost three hundred miles from San Francisco. She descended to nearly two hundred feet, lined up the Vega's nose in the ship's wake, and checked her course, confirming that her compass settings had pointed her in the right direction. Williams's charts had called for fourteen changes in her compass course, made about every hour, and had included three alternate routes—one to Los Angeles and one to San Francisco, as well as a mid-ocean change in case the weather turned bad. She ascended to fifteen hundred feet, anxious to see the California coast.

First, Pillar Point twenty-odd miles south of San Francisco appeared, and she deviated from her course to avoid a rainstorm, returned to her position, and arrived at Oakland Airport eighteen hours and fifteen minutes after leaving Honolulu, having logged 2,408 air miles. A crowd of ten thousand spectators rushed the field to greet her, dwarfing her plane as she cut the engine to keep the spinning propeller from harming the mob. This time, as she climbed from the cockpit, she looked pale and trembled some, exhausted from both the physical demands of the flight and the "mental hazard" created by the criticism she'd undergone in the islands for having embarked on the adventure in the first place. Following her transatlantic flights, she had received minor criticisms in letters and from only a couple of newspapers. This time, the criticism came ahead of her and made the flight more difficult. The harsh words had stung but her family provided encouragement: Putnam wired her, "Swell job" before boarding the *Lurline* with the Mantzes and Tissot to return home, and Amy Earhart told *The New York Times,* "I knew she would do it. Amelia and I like trying things. We like to see what a person can do."

In Oakland, her eyes bloodshot and sore from the streaming air and the strain of flying, Amelia denied rumors that she was giving up long-distance flights, but admitted she was tired and said, "I want sleep more than anything else." A physician examined her, declared her eyeball was bruised, and recommended rest. Her plans to continue on to Washington had been dashed by unfavorable weather in other parts of the country.

She ate a light supper of chicken broth, biscuits, and buttermilk, then she went to bed at an Oakland hotel with a guard at her door to ensure privacy.

Publicity over her propaganda contract with the sugar growers continued, and Amelia, in her article about the flight for *The New York Times,* did include the requisite glowing terms about the importance of Hawaii to the mainland. *The Nation* called the incident "sticky business," and suggested that Amelia should not have received the payment because "such transactions are generally regarded as corrupt," but indicated that Putnam had been at fault rather than she. The magazine cautioned her to remember she served as a model for young people and to behave more appropriately in the future. *The Aeroplane* of January 16, 1935, opined that she "proved herself equal to most male pilots and has shown that high order of courage which we have always known women to possess but seldom exhibit" but cautioned her to "find some less dangerous and more useful occupation."

Soaring

About a month after Amelia's triumphant Pacific flight, the Putnams attended a dinner at the home of airplane designer Paul Hammond. One of the guests at the New York party, British lord and traveler Sir Anthony Jenkinson, sat next to her, recorded his impressions in his diary, and later recounted in his book, *America Came My Way:* "So modest, so natural, and so feminine. . . . Clearly hers is a mental rather than a physical courage, giving effect, not to bulging muscles and a philosophy of reckless, senseless daring, but rather to abundant confidence, poise, and a firm, purposeful character."

He marveled at her navigation chart, two and a half feet long and eight inches wide, and marked with the proper instructions for hourly course adjustments, which she claimed made her work "dead easy."

She soon set off for yet another round of lectures throughout the Midwest, concluding with a speech in Washington to the National Geographic Society. Another tour, this time of New England, followed. But she longed to return to the sky and soon had a chance when on March 17, 1935, *The New York Times* reported she received an official invitation from the government of Mexico "to make a good-will flight" to Mexico City. She announced her intention to attempt a nonstop record flight. A comment made by her friend, pilot Wiley Post, who had successfully flown around the world in 1931 and 1933, helped her decide which route to take. She proposed to fly from Mexico City to New York in a straight line by cutting across the Gulf of Mexico, a seven-hundred-mile expanse of water. The straight-line route would save about an hour's flying time but she sought Post's advice on the idea.

Post said, "Amelia, don't do it. It's too dangerous."

She recalled: "I couldn't believe my ears. Did Wiley Post, the man who had braved every sort of hazard in his stratosphere flying, really regard a simple little flight from Mexico City to New York across the Gulf of Mexico as too hazardous? If so, I could scarcely wait to be on my way."

The Vega, located in New York, had to be flown to Los Angeles to be fitted with the appropriate tanks to carry the nearly five hundred gallons of fuel required for the flight. She had also agreed to test a new Lear radio compass, still in the experimental stage, earning the grand sum of one dollar per year from the Department of Commerce Air Bureau for her work as an experimental pilot.

She left the Union Air Terminal at Burbank, California, at 9:55 P.M. on Friday evening, April 19, determined to fly along the coast and then turn east to head toward the Mexican capital. Her takeoff "was lit by a generous moon which gilded the hills gloriously" but nearing the Gulf of California, she flew through a "white haze" that made it difficult to distinguish the sandy coast below from the misty clouds. Her engine began overheating, causing concern that she might have to land and ruin her plans for a nonstop flight. However, she determined the problem to be an incorrect pitch setting on the propeller, managed to reset it, and flew on, mostly at an altitude of about ten thousand feet.

Near Mazatlán, Mexico, a thousand miles from Burbank, she turned east, seeing "ruffles of mountains sloping upward into the high tableland of central Mexico." By using her compass, she had found the towns of Guadalajara and Tepic but about the time she was scheduled to arrive in the Mexican capital, she saw a railroad beneath her and realized she had flown off course. While reaching to check her map, a bug flew into her eye, making both her eyes water, diminishing her vision. She realized she had to land to get her bearings and circled a couple of times to determine an adequate site.

She landed in a cow pasture dotted with cactus and

managed to dodge the scattered but seemingly fearless cattle. Soon afterward, a number of cowboys, women, and children came running toward her. No one in the crowd spoke English and she could not speak Spanish, but they appeared to know who she was. She learned that she had touched down near the village of Nopala and her greeters managed to communicate well enough to point her toward Mexico City, about fifty miles distant. After ensuring they understood she needed a long, unobstructed path for takeoff, and shooing them from her makeshift runway, she climbed into the plane and again headed the Vega into the sky. The unforeseen delay cost her about a half hour and thwarted her plans for a nonstop journey.

Thirty minutes later she arrived at Mexico City's Valbuena Airport, setting a new speed record. *The New York Times* of April 21, 1935, reported the throng that greeted her was "the largest crowd at the airport since Colonel Charles A. Lindbergh arrived in 1927." Amelia said she hoped to make the flight again and to "try to do a better job of flying nonstop to New York." Ten thousand people streamed through the lines of soldiers to catch sight of her. Her husband had flown ahead from New York and met her at the airport, and Foreign Minister Emilio Portes Gil greeted her with flowers.

During her time in Mexico, she received a medal from the Mexican Geographic Society, attended a jai alai game, and toured the floating gardens of Xochimilco. She hoped to speak with the women of Mexico, especially those who supported themselves through their farm labor, but had to be content with a wealthier group. As her free hours dwindled, she made plans for the return trip to the States, the first nonstop flight between the two cities. According to *The Times,* only one other pilot, Mexican Captain Emilio Carranza, had attempted to fly nonstop between New York and Mexico City and he had been killed after encountering severe thunderstorms and crashing his plane in New Jersey.

She would again be taking off in an airplane weighing nearly three tons, loaded with 470 gallons of fuel, but this takeoff presented a wholly new dilemma. The eight-thousand-foot elevation of Mexico City meant that her cumbersome craft needed more runway space to build speed for takeoff. Since the length required was more than the runways of the cities could provide, to assist her, the Mexican Army cleared a three-mile path for her in the dry bed of Lake Texcoco. Weather delays forced her to wait more than a week before she could take off.

To help finance the flight, Putnam had seized upon the idea of Amelia's carrying collectible stamps along with her. Mexican President Lázaro Cárdenas authorized 780 Mexican airmail stamps to be imprinted *"Amelia Earhart Vuelo de Buena Voluntad Mexico 1935"* (Amelia Earhart Good-Will Flight Mexico 1935). The stamps were divided among several groups: 480 were presented to the International Postal Union at Berne, Switzerland; 24 to Mexican philatelic associations; 35

to the Mexico post office; and one was saved for the philatelist President Franklin Roosevelt. However, Putnam kept the remaining 240, according to a later report in *Newsweek* magazine, effectively cornering the market and driving the price to $100 each, drawing the anger of collectors, who hoped to obtain the stamps, normally costing less than one cent. Amelia had carried signed and numbered stamp covers with her previously on both her ocean journeys, and some of the covers for the Mexico City expedition fetched prices as high as $175. Criticism erupted over this plan, dredging up her husband's previous questionable promotional schemes, including the Hawaiian sugar matter. Putnam denied any wrongdoing and planned to sell the stamps in the United States and Mexico to pay part of Amelia's flight expenses.

On the morning of May 8, 1935, Putnam received word from meteorologist "Doc" Kimball in New York City that the weather was favorable. Amelia thereupon requested that Charles Baughan, a Lockheed pilot and Mexico City air charter service owner, oversee the fueling of the Vega, which had been flown from the city to Lake Texcoco. At 4:00 A.M., her interpreter drove her to the lake bed where the Pan American mechanic performed his finishing adjustments in the dim illumination provided by the headlights of several automobiles and a waning moon. Before she climbed into the cockpit, Amelia, clad in a flannel shirt, checked tie, and trousers, told reporters, "This is the most hazardous takeoff of my experience. I shall probably have to taxi at least a mile and a half." She estimated a sixteen-hour trip but refrained from mentioning the most dangerous part of her journey—crossing the Gulf of Mexico.

Just after 6:00 A.M. she settled inside the Vega and gunned the engine. According to *The Times,* she lumbered down the lake bed for nearly three miles in a four-minute takeoff, although she later estimated she needed only a little more than a mile of the runway to become airborne. She later wrote of the event: "But all I had to do was keep the plane moving in a straight line and hold it on the ground until we'd built up a speed well over a hundred miles an hour—then it just flew itself into the air."

She climbed to ten thousand feet to clear the mountains, seeing the peak of the Popocatépetl volcano in the south and "a fairyland of beauty" below her, and after flying past the mountains, encountered clouds, turned to the northeast at Tampico, and headed toward New Orleans. Along the way she sipped tomato juice and ate a hard-boiled egg and a small chicken sandwich. She had brought along additional sandwiches and boiled eggs as well as water and a thermos of hot chocolate. In contrast to her other long-distance flights, this one, she said, was "marked by a delightful precision." The radio compass worked well, and she was unhampered by mechanical malfunctions. She bucked headwinds over the gulf, but a tailwind favored her as she neared New York, and her speed averaged 151 miles per hour. Along the way, people gathered at airports to catch a glimpse of her flying past, and she kept in continuous radio communication over the states. When she flew over Hoover Airport, in Washington, her friend Eugene Vidal, director of the Air Commerce Bureau of the Department of Commerce, radioed, "You've done a splendid job, so come down." She elected to continue to Newark, having already set a record of thirteen hours, five minutes, and fifty-two seconds between the two national capitals, shaving fourteen hours from Lindbergh's earlier flight between those cities in the much slower *Spirit of St. Louis.*

At 10:28 P.M., having flown 2,185 miles, she landed at the New Jersey airport where a crowd of thousands, including Putnam and "Doc" Kimball, awaited her. She told reporters she had not carried along any good-luck charms with her. "I prefer good mechanical work to rabbits' feet," she said.

In their efforts to help protect her from the crowd, the police nearly split her in two. One officer held her right arm and another took hold of her left leg, and each started walking in an opposite direction. Amelia said she felt "a fleeting taste of the tortures of the rack" but the cops soon discovered their folly and took greater care with their charge.

After ensuring that the Vega was secured, she and Putnam headed to their city apartment in the Hotel

Seymour in New York. The next day, one thousand people were allowed to see the Vega, which had been housed in the Standard Oil Company's hangar at the airport.

In early June 1935 Purdue University President Edward C. Elliott announced that Amelia would serve as a career counselor for women at the university. Women made up more than thirteen percent of the student body and Elliott, who had spoken with Amelia in 1934 after her presentation at the "Women and the Changing World" conference sponsored by the *New York Herald Tribune,* believed that her zestful approach to life and her straightforward attitudes about women and careers would provide helpful and practical guidance to female students. Of her selection he said, "Miss Earhart represents better than any other young woman of this generation the spirit and courageous skill of what may be called the new pioneering." She would earn $2,000 annually for her work, which included staying on the campus for about a month each year.

Soon after the Purdue announcement, Amelia underwent surgery at Cedars of Lebanon Hospital in California to help her recover from the chronic sinusitis she suffered. She recuperated at the home of friends of G.P.'s in Oceanside, California.

She could not stay away from airplanes for long, and before a month had passed she was frequenting the

Union Airfield and working with Paul Mantz, the striking stunt pilot with the thin mustache, slicked-back hair, and movie-star looks who had served as her technical adviser for her Pacific flight. While working on plans for the creation of the Earhart-Mantz Flying School, they impulsively decided to enter the Bendix Race. Mantz analyzed the pilots and the planes competing in the event and decided that Amelia and her Vega could likely place fifth and pay their expenses with the $500 cash prize for that position.

She entered the race, and on August 30, 1935, Mantz and his mechanic, Al Menasco, rode along with her, playing cards and sipping whiskey in the back of the Vega on the route from Los Angeles to Cleveland. As Mantz predicted, Amelia came in fifth. Winner Ben Howard, a race plane designer flying in a Howard Racer, averaged 239 miles per hour and made the trip in eight hours, thirty-three minutes, and sixteen seconds to receive the $4,500 prize.

G.P. joined them on the return flight to Los Angeles. The Putnams had purchased a house in Toluca Lake, California, and the race gave Amelia a pleasant breather from other obligations. In 1935 she gave 135 lectures during a nine-month tour, including one at the United States Naval Academy in Annapolis, Maryland, where she was the first woman to address the midshipmen. She also received the Harmon Trophy, earning recognition as the nation's outstanding air woman. (Following her transatlantic solo, she shared the Harmon award for the

World's Outstanding Woman Aviator, with pilot Jean Batten, who had successfully completed a solo flight across the South Atlantic.)

At Purdue that fall, she ruffled the feathers of some of the more staid members of the faculty with her informal approach but impressed the young women students with her talks. Although she could not visit individually with each female student, she stayed at one of the dormitories and joined the girls in impromptu evening conversations in their rooms, sitting on the floor with them. She ate in the dining room and began a new cafeteria trend when she selected buttermilk for her beverage. She urged the Purdue women to examine their reasons for attending college, prompted them to consider whether they were taking classes on their own initiative or because a relative thought they should, and provoked similar discussions about careers. "Too much emphasis, it seems to me, has been placed on learning a skill without finding out whether the student has a natural bent or talent for that particular work, or whether the working world needs that person when he or she is trained," she said.

She prepared a survey, discovered that ninety-two percent of the young women wanted a career, and advised them to think of the effect their choice would have on their future husbands and families. (She had once confided to her sister that she had not had children because she decided that with her flying career and other obligations she could not give a young child proper attention.)

She cautioned them not to confuse sexual interest with love, which required a deeper commitment from both partners. "Surely we must have something more to contribute to marriage than our bodies," she said. "We must earn true respect and equal rights from men by accepting responsibility."

She encouraged the coeds to explore their interests, reiterating the views she'd expressed in *American Magazine* following her transatlantic solo: "Young people and old people, too, are too timid about experimenting, trying their little adventures, flying their own Atlantics. Step out! Try the job you are interested in! Use the talents which give you joy! There's plenty of time."

Her friendship with Paul Mantz made headlines in March 1936 when Mantz's wife, Myrtle, sued him for divorce and named Amelia as a corespondent in the lawsuit. The *Los Angeles Times* carried the front-page story, reporting that Myrtle sued Mantz on the grounds of "mental cruelty" and that he had countered with similar charges. Mantz maintained that Amelia had hired him as a technical adviser and had purchased stock in his company, United Air Services, Limited, and although she had stayed in the Mantzes' home for a month and had visited again at another time for several days, they had not been alone in the house together. Myrtle had confided to a friend she was "insanely jealous and upset," and wanted Amelia to "take her clothes and leave our house" so that she and her husband "would have a much better chance of getting along." Both

Amelia and G.P. wrote to her mother, Amy, dismissing the woman's claim as simply the action of an envious spouse and a greedy lawyer, the situation exacerbated by Amelia's widespread fame. She continued to rely upon Mantz's advice concerning her flight plans and her plane.

In her zestful pursuit of new aviation experiences, Amelia decided to try an around-the-world flight. Although Wiley Post had already twice successfully completed such an adventure in 1931 and 1933, she could become the first woman pilot to circle the earth. (During Post's third attempt at a world flight, he and passenger Will Rogers, the celebrated humorist, were killed when their airplane crashed at Point Barrow, Alaska, on August 15, 1935.) Post's flights had concentrated on speed, so to make her attempt differ from his, she planned to concentrate on distance, flying "the world at its waistline"—following the equator. With the help of Mantz and Purdue University, she found a new craft to make the flight possible.

Mantz chose a sleek, all-metal, Lockheed Electra 10E, equipped with two Pratt and Whitney S3H-1 engines of 550 horsepower each and a retractable landing gear, capable of achieving a speed of more than two hundred miles per hour with a flight ceiling of 27,500 feet. That fall, a private donor contributed $50,000 and additional donations were received from industrialist Vincent Bendix, pharmaceutical magnate J. K. Lilly, and several corporations including Western Electric and

Goodyear for Amelia's new $80,000 airplane. She would use this "flying laboratory," purchased through the Purdue Research Foundation, to study how changes in altitude and air pressure affected pilots, how diet and preflight consumption of alcohol altered their performance, and what in-flight physiological changes occurred and how they differed in men and women.

On July 22, 1936, she took a first test flight in the Electra, copiloting the shiny and sophisticated ship with Lockheed's test pilot, Elmer McLeod, at the Union Air Terminal in Los Angeles. She said the plane was equipped with "over a hundred dials and gadgets which I either have to look at or twiddle." Among these instruments were a Sperry Gyro-pilot, an early form of automatic pilot control, as well as a Bendix radio direction finder and new communications equipment from Western Electric. The airplane would undergo additional tests in Los Angeles before she took it to Purdue University for more flight experiments.

In September she entered the Electra in the Bendix Race, flying the route from New York to Los Angeles with Helen Richey of Pittsburgh, the first female commercial transport pilot in the nation. Richey had worked for Central Air Lines but was forced to resign when she could not gain entrance into the all-male pilots union. Amelia had defended the twenty-five-year-old Richey during the dispute but the rules had not been changed.

The two women were the third contestants to take off from New York's Floyd Bennett Field on September

4, 1936. Other female competitors included Louise Thaden, winner of the 1929 Women's Air Derby, and her partner, pilot Blanche Noyes, who had also competed in the women's race, and Laura Ingalls, the 1934 winner of the Harmon Trophy recognizing the world's outstanding female flier. Amelia told reporters for *The New York Times* she expected to make just one stop to refuel in Kansas City, Kansas. Not long after takeoff, the navigator's hatch blew open and the women pulled it closed and secured it with a rag. At their refueling stop in Kansas City, the hatch was repaired but a faulty fuel system cost them time. Even so, they were among the lucky ones who completed the race; several other pilots in this competition crashed, sustaining personal injuries and ruining their planes. The Earhart-Richey team placed fifth and won $500. Laura Ingalls placed second in a Lockheed Orion. Winners Louise Thaden and Blanche Noyes made the cross-country journey in a Beechcraft C17R with a 420-horsepower Wright engine in fourteen hours, fifty-five minutes, and one second, claiming the $4,500 prize for first place as well as the additional $2,500 women's award, the first females to win the male-dominated Bendix Race.

World

Of her decision to fly "the world at its waist-line" Amelia wrote, "Here was shining adventure, beckoning with new experiences, added knowledge of flying, of peoples—of myself."

Her route, roughly following the equator and an estimated distance of twenty-seven thousand miles, would be the longest world flight ever attempted. It would begin in Oakland, include stops at Honolulu, at a speck on the map of the Pacific called Howland Island, at New Guinea, Australia, India, East Africa, and Brazil before concluding in the United States.

Putnam obtained the necessary permissions for the numerous foreign countries where she would land—something they had neglected in her flights to Ireland and to Mexico. He sought assistance from Eleanor Roosevelt, the State Department, the Department of the

Interior, and President Roosevelt, who authorized the United States Navy to assist. The Standard Oil Company agreed to stock their fuel depots at designated stops along Amelia's route.

Lockheed mechanic Bo McKneely kept the Electra NR 16020 fit for flight, and Clarence Belinn, top engineer at National Airways, created a cross-feed fuel tank design to increase the fuel efficiency in the wings with the operational valve located in the cockpit. Fitted with twelve gas tanks—six in the wings and six in the fuselage—the Electra could carry as much as 1,150 gallons of fuel, giving the ship a flight capacity of four thousand miles. Amelia employed Paul Mantz as technical adviser at $100 per hour, and the stunt pilot installed a Link trainer in his Burbank hangar so she could practice instrument flying there. She had flown the 1936 Bendix Race in part to gain more time in the Electra, and had spent five weeks of intense flight training with Lockheed test pilot Elmer McLeod and Mantz. Even so, she continued her lecture schedule, took on additional work helping G.P. with preflight tour details, studied geography and weather throughout the world to better acquaint herself with the countries she would fly to, and even made time to engage in some campaigning for the Democrats during the presidential election year.

Friction developed between Mantz and Putnam over equipment and costs. Mantz thought Putnam was too concerned with expenses, neglecting safety to save money. G.P. and Amelia had invested almost everything they owned in the world expedition. One of the costs they had to defray involved the construction of an airstrip on tiny Howland Island in the Pacific Ocean, partially funded by the government. Before Amelia embarked on her journey, Putnam arranged for another batch of stamp covers to be carried with her and postmarked in Oakland on her departure, in either India or Africa during her trip, and upon her return. The covers, sold by Gimbel's department store, were priced at $2.50 each or $5.00 each with Amelia's autograph. He decided to sell the Vega, scheduled $500 post-flight lectures, and contracted with the *New York Herald Tribune* for Amelia's first-person story of the flight.

Clarence S. Williams, the retired naval officer who had constructed charts for her Honolulu to Oakland flight, mapped her route. Captain Harry Manning, an officer of the United States Lines and the skipper of the SS *Roosevelt*, who had become acquainted with Amelia on her return to America following the *Friendship* flight, agreed to serve as her navigator and would accompany her from California to Australia. After that, she would fly solo.

Mantz had supplied the Electra with a navigator's table in the rear section of the airplane, and the steersman could reach the cockpit via a "catwalk" built across the massive fuel tanks, but most communication between the pilot and star-watcher would occur by sending notes back and forth along a fishing line attached to a bamboo pole. The navigator's table had a glass inset for easy viewing of the stabilized aperiodic compass located below, and nearby stood chronometers, altimeter, airspeed and drift indicators, pelorus or a compass sighting device, temperature gauge and a marine sextant. While Amelia would rely upon her navigator to provide accurate celestial navigation, she would use the dead-reckoning method, calculating her route by reading maps, spotting landmarks below, and using her magnetic compass to sight her destinations. The Bendix radio direction finder and radio contacts with ships at sea and shore-based stations would provide additional flight guidance.

In November 1936 Amelia met Jacqueline Cochran, a cosmetics entrepreneur who had begun to make a name for herself as an aviator. Cochran was married to former utilities tycoon Floyd Odlum, a donor to Amelia's world flight, and during a cross-country trip together in the Electra, the two women discovered a shared affinity for extrasensory perception. During a stay at the Odlums' Indio, California, estate, the two women tested their psychic skills by attempting to locate a missing airliner. Cochran gave details and the location of the aircraft, lost between Los Angeles and Salt Lake City, and they verified her story by calling Paul Mantz in California who looked up the names and locations on an air chart and called them back. When Cochran used her skills to envision the location of another downed plane a few weeks later, she convinced Amelia that E.S.P. could help her if she needed rescuing during her forthcoming airplane journey.

Amelia relaxed at the Indio estate, swimming and riding horses, to prepare for the flight. Jackie Cochran questioned whether Harry Manning's navigational skills would be as keen in the air as on the sea and suggested that she fly from Los Angeles over the Pacific near the California coast, then circle for a while to disorient the navigator and see if he could guide them safely back to their starting point. Amelia did this, and they arrived back at the coast midway between Los Angeles and San Francisco. She liked Manning and he had already arranged a leave of absence from his shipboard duties, but Paul Mantz, who shared Cochran's concerns about the critical navigation question, suggested a backup navigator be hired.

Throughout the end of the year rumors circulated that Amelia was planning a global trip of some kind, but she denied them, waiting until February 11, 1937, to make her public announcement at the Barclay Hotel in New York.

In March she readied for takeoff but bad weather delayed her. Fred Noonan, an American-born former British merchant marine and onetime navigator for Pan American Airways, joined her crew around this time. Noonan's extensive experience included work as navigation teacher and navigator on the Pacific Clipper flying boats in addition to mapping air routes throughout the South Pacific, the Philippines, and Hong Kong. However, he was said to have been dismissed from his position with Pan Am because of his heavy drinking.

On March 17, 1937, Amelia and Mantz, together with Manning and Noonan, left Oakland in the Electra. The beginning of the world flight drew little press attention as weather delays had dampened the enthusiasm of reporters and spectators, although a photographer from the *San Francisco Chronicle*, flying in another airplane, managed to capture a shot of the Electra in flight as it passed over the new Golden Gate Bridge, then nearing completion. Newspapers attributed an excellent takeoff in just 1,897 feet of runway in the hefty Electra, filled with 947 gallons of fuel and weighing more than six tons, to Amelia, although Earhart biographer Doris Rich states that Mantz flew the plane. She flew to Hawaii taking hourly breaks with Mantz taking the controls.

Mantz used the direction finder to locate Makapuu Point on Oahu prior to their landing, and again took the controls to set the craft down. In Don Dwiggins's book, *Hollywood Pilot*, Mantz recalled, "I went around Makapuu Point and then crossed Wheeler Field. I wrapped it around in a steep bank to check the wind sock. AE yelled 'Don't! Don't!' She was very fatigued and kind of exuberant. She calmed down when I made a normal approach pattern and we landed." They set down at Wheeler Field on Oahu, at 5:40 A.M. Hawaiian time, breaking a record for speed, clocking fifteen hours and forty-seven minutes for the more than twenty-four-hundred-mile trip.

In Hawaii, she rested rather than continue as planned on her eighteen-hundred-mile journey to Howland Island. She stayed at Chris Holmes's residence, skipping the engagement party for Mantz and his fiancée, who was already in the islands.

The next day, March 20, a series of potential mishaps were narrowly averted before she climbed into the cockpit. The Pratt and Whitney mechanic in Honolulu discovered that the propeller bearings had nearly gone dry, and Mantz claimed that 590 gallons of gas trucked from Wheeler Field to the takeoff site at Luke Field near Pearl Harbor had been contaminated. He caught the mistake before the fuel had been loaded onto the Electra, making a deal with the military for use of their high-octane aviation fuel instead. Amelia arrived at the field in the early-morning hours but waited until dawn to take off.

As she guided the Electra down the three-thousand-foot concrete runway, the airplane, filled with nine hundred gallons of gas, began swerving. She gunned the left engine, opposite the direction of the sway, but could not gain control of the craft. The airplane ground-looped, damaging undercarriage, landing gear, right wing, and propeller, coming to rest on the right engine mount. She switched off the ignition to avert a fire but was shaken by the accident. No one aboard was injured, and Army personnel later spoke of her calm demeanor after the incident.

She first attributed the wreck to a wet spot on the pavement, then blamed a blown tire, and later thought the right shock absorber on the landing gear collapsed. The exact cause of the accident was never ascertained but the extreme weight of the airplane was thought to have contributed to it. Mantz, who had been among the sparse crowd watching, thought she may have overcompensated with the throttle, a bad habit she had formed and one that he had tried to correct.

Putnam wired encouragement, saying that her decision to continue or quit was "equally jake with me." She told the press that the accident merely postponed her trip and later wrote, "Nothing which happened changed my attitude toward the original project. Indeed, I felt better about the ship and its equipment than I ever did before. I was eager to fly it again." She returned to the States on the liner *Malolo*.

Harry Manning returned to work rather than continuing on with Amelia but much later confided to friends that he had lost confidence in her piloting skills. The stamp covers were held at Honolulu until further arrangements could be made for them to be carried during her next attempt; the Coast Guard and Navy ships, specially posted along Amelia's planned route, returned to regular duty. The mechanic chosen to overhaul the airplane's engines in Karachi had flown from London to India to be prepared for their arrival, and upon receiving news of the accident, returned to England. The Electra, meantime, was crated and sent the next week on the liner *Lurline* to the Lockheed plant in California for repairs, which would take almost three months and cost twenty-five thousand dollars.

Amelia arrived in Los Angeles on March 23, 1937, where she faced a daunting and costly task, compressing a year's work into a scant nine weeks of time. During the months spent repairing the Electra, weather conditions around the world changed, monsoons and dust storms threatening some regions along her original route. After consulting with chart expert Clarence Williams and top meteorologists, she reversed the direction of her flight. She had to rearrange the previously granted international permissions, set up different fueling stops, and ensure that mechanics would be available at designated stops along the way to tune up the plane's twin engines, as well as reacquaint herself with the alternate course with help from Noonan. As she worked out those details, she also supervised the rebuilding work on her airplane.

Industrialist Vincent Bendix, her friend Floyd Odlum, and polar explorer Richard Byrd, along with several others, donated funds, and G.P. raised some, while Amelia worked numerous public appearances into her already dense schedule to help pay the $25,000 required to make the new flight arrangements. She later wrote, "I more-or-less mortgaged the future. Without regret, however, for what are futures for?"

In late May she flew the Electra to Miami on "a practical shake-down flight" with Putnam, navigator Noonan who had replaced Manning, and mechanic McKneely riding along, and planned to begin her world tour from Florida. Mantz learned of her test flight while attending a St. Louis air show. She later wrote that because of the publicity surrounding the Hawaii takeoff,

"I thought it would be a pleasant change just to slip away without comment." She had spoken to one reporter, her friend Carl Allen of the *New York Herald Tribune,* telling him, "I have a feeling that there is just about one more good trip in my system" and she admitted that she planned to retire from flying long distance upon her return. She asked that he not reveal her plans until after her world flight was completed.

In Tucson one of the plane's engines backfired and spurted flames but the craft's internal extinguisher quenched the fire and mechanic McKneely replaced the burnt rubber seals. In Miami, worried that excess weight may have led to her Hawaii crash, Amelia discarded items she deemed unnecessary, including the Morse code key and the 250-foot trailing radio antenna. She carried only one suitcase filled with "five shirts, two pairs of slacks, a change of shoes, a light working coverall, and a trick weightless raincoat, plus the minimum of toilet articles."

On June 1, at 5:56 A.M., Amelia began her second attempt at the world flight with five hundred people watching the silver Electra's departure from Miami's Municipal Airport. Newsreels and photographs depicted a smiling pilot, kneeling atop a shiny wing, dressed in a white shirt with a checked scarf and trousers, holding her leather jacket and wearing lace-up oxfords, talking to a cheerful-appearing Putnam, who stood on the ground, clasping her hand. Noonan climbed into the Electra, Amelia followed, and Putnam stepped aboard on the wing, leaning inside the cockpit to give his wife a farewell kiss. Just before the wheel chocks were removed, while the engines warmed up, she waved to David Putnam. This time, the Electra climbed into the air easily, and Amelia and Noonan headed toward San Juan, Puerto Rico. A Miami radio station broadcast hourly weather reports for Amelia's benefit, and she was required to broadcast her position every half hour.

They arrived in San Juan at 1:10 P.M., almost exactly in agreement with Noonan's estimate, and ate a lunch prepared by the wife of the local manager of Pan American Airways. Although the acting governor, Menendez Ramos, offered them accommodations, they opted to stay at the home of Clara Livingston, Puerto Rico's only female pilot, twenty miles from town. Amelia wrote, "We wanted quiet and sleep. When politely possible, it was helpful to avoid functions and people—even the pleasantest people, for meeting and talking to them adds immeasurably to the fatigue factor, nervous and physical."

From San Juan, they flew to Caripito, Venezuela, flying over the "green mountains of Puerto Rico" at eight thousand feet where clouds resembled "white scrambled eggs" and the Venezuelan coast offered Amelia her first glimpse of a jungle, an area she considered the most dangerous for pilots. (She had once confided in young Gore Vidal, the future novelist, that she feared being lost forever among the trees.) From Caripito, they traveled to Paramaribo, capital of Dutch Guiana, where they stayed overnight before flying to Fortaleza, Brazil, a ten-hour journey over 960 miles of dense jungle and 370 miles of water, during which they crossed the equator for the first time. They stayed for a day to do laundry and rest at the Excelsior Hotel in Fortaleza while Pan American Airways mechanics repaired a minor gas leak, changed the oil, and greased the Electra's engine.

Amelia's punishing routine included rising hours before dawn to conduct preflight checks of the ship, then averaging six hours of flight, landing in a foreign country, writing her daily dispatch for the *New York Herald Tribune* and a note to G.P., and reviewing the next day's flight plan before retiring for a frequently short, fitful sleep.

From Fortaleza, at 4:50 A.M., they took off for Natal, Brazil, completing the 270-mile flight a little before 7:00 A.M., planning to fly across the South Atlantic that evening. After Amelia consulted French airmail pilots who flew the nineteen-hundred-mile sea route biweekly, she discovered they preferred early-morning takeoffs and changed her schedule, but strong crosswinds the next morning blocked use of the paved runway. In the predawn darkness, she and Noonan, using flashlights, walked an alternate grass runway searching for impediments that might endanger their takeoff before attempting the perilous takeoff in the weighty Electra.

Thirteen hours and twelve minutes later, they arrived in Saint-Louis, Senegal, Africa. Although they met an Air France mail plane en route, they could not communicate with it because Amelia had only her voice phone and the French plane used telegraphic code. Rather than Saint-Louis, their planned destination had been Dakar, but Amelia had ignored Noonan's advice to turn south along the African coast and flew north instead, pulling them 163 miles off course. She later admitted her error, and they made the short trip to Dakar the next morning, staying with the governor general and attending a dinner and an Aero Club reception while the plane's engines were checked.

The African crossing, a distance of 4,350 miles split into four flights, required early-morning takeoffs to take advantage of cooler hours when the heavier air provided more lift for the plane. Even so, the metal of the fuselage often grew too hot to touch, they encountered turbulence when airborne, and Amelia wrote that the stifling air was so debilitating they sometimes neglected to record the cockpit temperatures. From Dakar, they traveled to Fort-Lamy in Chad, El Fasher and Khartoum, Sudan. Noonan struggled with inaccurate regional maps and a dearth of landmarks and decided oceans were easier to navigate than Africa. From Khartoum, they flew to Massawa, arriving during the evening with the temperature at one hundred degrees. To take advantage of a better runway, they moved from Massawa, Ethiopia, to Assab, and loaded the airplane with more 87 octane fuel there. At each of Amelia's destinations, Standard Oil provided fifty-gallon drums of fuel, stamped with her name in bright colors. Extra precautions were taken, including filtering fuel through a chamois cloth to prevent contamination.

From Assab, they crossed the Red Sea en route to Karachi, India, passing over Baluchistan on the Persian border and the mouth of the Persian Gulf. Foreigners in Arab lands sparked suspicion, but Amelia carried a letter written in Arabic to explain her mission and to protect her and Noonan from harm. They carried sun helmets plus "a generous supply of water in canteens, concentrated foods, a small land compass, and very heavy walking shoes" in case they had to land in the desert. When they arrived safely in Karachi after a 1,920-mile, thirteen-hour-and-ten-minute flight, they learned that the nonstop crossing of the Red Sea to India was the first ever made.

Even though she reported to her readers in the United States that she and Noonan were in "robust health," to protect the health of natives, both they and the Electra were often fumigated by officials in the course of their journey. She wrote, "Every time the plane landed, attendants with flit guns or more elaborate contraptions flung open the door and began squirting. Having been in a yellow fever district, Fred and I were suspects, warnings of our coming having been sent on ahead."

In Karachi, a malfunctioning fuel-mixture gauge, which prevented Amelia from knowing how much gas the right engine consumed, was repaired and the engines replaced with spares shipped to the city especially for the flight and serviced by Imperial Airlines mechanics. She took the stamp covers to the Karachi post office to be canceled, visited with an interviewer from the local press, and rode a camel, remarking that the animals "should have shock absorbers." She also spoke to G.P. on the telephone for the second time on her trip, for the most part a brief, businesslike conversation, but when he asked if she was having fun, said, "You betja! It's a grand trip. We'll do it again, together, sometime."

On June 17 she and Noonan departed Karachi for the 1,390-mile trip to Calcutta. Numerous railroads throughout central India aided their navigation on this route, but a heavy haze obscured their view at times. At five thousand feet, they encountered an unexpected hazard when black eagles flew near "oblivious of the Electra and giving its pilot some very bad moments." Both airplane and birds survived the meeting without harm. Later, as she and Noonan flew over Agra, she lamented not having had enough time to stop and visit the Taj Mahal. They arrived in Calcutta in a rainstorm that cleared soon after they set down, allowing them to take afternoon tea outside near the plane.

The takeoff from Calcutta was made "precarious" after rains had soaked the ground, and the cumbersome airplane barely cleared trees at the runway's end. After trying to reach Rangoon, monsoons forced them to land in Akyab, Burma. The next day they reached Rangoon, but their plans to fly on to Bangkok were thwarted by the unrelenting rains. During the layover, Amelia visited the Shwedagon Pagoda, delighting in the diverse cultures of Burmese, Indians, and Chinese and those practicing varying religions—Christians, Hindus, Muslims, and Buddhists—dwelling together in the city. Noonan refused to remove his shoes and socks to enter the Buddhist temple, and Amelia later wrote it was "the first time on the trip Fred Noonan failed me."

From Rangoon they flew to Singapore and Bandoeng (Bandung, Indonesia), delayed again by monsoons. She spoke to G.P. again, telling him she planned to arrive in the States on the Fourth of July. On June 24 she and Noonan flew 350 miles to Soerabaja, Java, but returned to Bandoeng because several of the Electra's fuel indicators—the fuel analyzer, flow and generator gauges—were malfunctioning. Amelia cabled her husband about the delay, including a vague reference about them not being ready to proceed. Noonan had been drinking while she battled exhaustion, nausea, diarrhea, and airsickness from the gasoline fumes concentrated in the tiny cockpit.

On June 27 they left Bandoeng, flying to Koepang on Timor Island, and the next day to Port Darwin, Australia, and on to Lae, New Guinea, on June 30. There she wrote, "Not much more than a month ago I was on the other shore of the Pacific, looking westward. This evening, I looked eastward over the Pacific. In those fast-moving days which have intervened, the whole width of the world has passed behind us—except this broad ocean. I shall be glad when we have the hazards of its navigation behind us."

Lost

melia awoke on Friday, July 2, 1937, to the predawn promise of another stifling day with few cooling breezes to provide relief from the heat and thus little help to lift her hefty Electra into the air. Visibility was good but the forecast predicted partly cloudy conditions and rain squalls, and head winds of up to fifteen knots. In preparation for the forthcoming 2,556-mile flight to Howland Island, she and Fred Noonan had spent the previous day eliminating all excess weight from the airplane—even discarding personal baggage and papers—to make room for the thousand gallons of fuel necessary to power their craft down the three-thousand-foot runway at Lae, New Guinea, and for an estimated eighteen-hour journey across the Pacific. Although she sent home a treasured bracelet, she wore the watch London department store

owner Gordon Selfridge had given her after her successful 1932 transatlantic solo. Selfridge had first given the
watch to De Hane Segrave, a well-known athlete killed
in a boat racing accident, and after his death, Segrave's
family returned it. When Selfridge presented the time-
piece to Amelia, she gave him the silver watch she had
worn both times she flew across the Atlantic.

Time differences figured into this longest leg of the
world flight since the Electra would cross two time
zones plus the International Dateline to arrive at Howland Island where it was still only Thursday. They had
chosen to follow Greenwich Mean Time, beginning
their flight at zero hours so the elapsed flying time
would be easily comprehended. That meant a 10:00 A.M.
departure from Lae so they could spot Howland Island
from the air during the daylight hours.

She and Noonan had traveled twenty-two thousand
miles around the world but needed to log seven thousand more to complete the route they had charted. The
trip to Howland was the first leg of three passing over
the tropical waters of the Pacific, with flights to Hawaii
and then to California, of eighteen hundred miles and
twenty-four hundred miles respectively, yet before
them. Despite the physical and mental toll exacted by
earlier segments of the world tour, Amelia and her navigator faced the most difficult task of their journey in
attempting to find Howland in the midst of the vast
blue ocean. The island, just twenty feet high, two miles
long, and a half-mile wide, had been placed under the

Department of Interior's jurisdiction in 1936, and a special landing strip had been built there for Amelia, to be used later for military purposes. Noonan's skills in reading the stars, together with his expertise with the navigational equipment on board the Electra, and her own abilities in using dead reckoning while she piloted the plane would be taxed to their limits.

Amelia's face, most often cast with a pleasant, serene smile, now showed her weariness, appearing creased with frown lines in some photographs, her cheeks sunken and eyes puffy. Noonan had been drinking. She had mentioned in her report to the *New York Herald Tribune* that they would not arrive in the United States by the Fourth of July as planned because of radio problems, Noonan's difficulty in setting the chronometers properly, and unfavorable weather conditions. The chronometers required precision because a fifteen-second error would lead to a one-mile difference in Noonan's calculations of position. Over the long distance they intended to fly, such a seemingly small mistake could amount to sending them many miles off course over the ocean with no hope of finding Howland.

She had spoken to G.P. only sporadically during the trip, in Puerto Rico, Karachi, Calcutta, Bandoeng, and Soerabaja, Indonesia, and otherwise they had communicated through cables. The messages took twenty-four hours to reach her because they had forwarded them to her from Samoa. She knew he had set up a radio interview for her on the night of July 5, expecting her to arrive in California by then. Communications now would be sent through the United States Coast Guard cutter *Itasca,* stationed at Howland Island to provide radio support and help guide her safely to her destination, which was, as she had written, "a fantastically tiny target."

Local pilot Bertie Heath, who ferried supplies to the Bulolo, New Guinea, gold mines in his Junkers trimotor, was flying near Lae that morning of July 2, watched Amelia's departure from the air, her first takeoff with the Electra filled nearly to its maximum fuel capacity. The airplane, with no helpful wind to provide important lift for the wings, broke away from the ground about fifty feet from the end of the runway, then disappeared behind the twenty-five-foot drop-off that led to the Huon Gulf, flying so close to the water that "the propellers were throwing spray," Heath told pilot and author Ann Pellegreno. Amelia flew near the sea for several miles, taking advantage of the cushion of air existing just above the water before she began climbing.

Seven hours and twenty minutes after departing Lae, she reported her position about twenty miles southwest of the Nukumanu Islands, north of the Solomon group. Harry Balfour, the radio operator for New Guinea Airways, received her transmission, the only time in her flight that she successfully broadcast her position. She still had seventeen hundred miles of ocean to cover to reach Howland. Balfour received another, weaker report from the Electra about forty minutes later indicating she was on course and flying at twelve thousand feet altitude. Both of her broadcasts had been transmitted on the daytime frequency of her radio equipment, 6210 kilocycles, but she informed Balfour she was changing to the nighttime frequency of 3105 kilocycles so she could contact the United States Coast Guard cutter *Itasca*, stationed at Howland.

Three hours and ten minutes after she gave Balfour her position, residents of Nauru Island heard her report that she saw a ship or lights, presumably the naval auxiliary tug, USS *Ontario*, standing 423 miles from the Nukumanu Islands, and stationed there for Amelia's protection. Although the ship broadcast the homing signal "N" in Morse code as she had earlier requested by cable, radio operators on board did not receive a response, nor did they hear her transmissions, and the crew, posted to watch specifically for the Electra, did not see the plane pass over. Another ship, the USS *Myrtlebank*, was steaming toward Nauru and was forty-four miles north of Amelia's planned route, the only other vessel in possible range.

The commander of the *Itasca*, Warner K. Thompson, received two reports of her Lae departure time from San Francisco, one of them erroneous, but had not heard from her. He estimated that her trip to Howland would take more than nineteen hours, accounting for head winds that were stronger than Amelia had expected in calculating her estimated time of eighteen hours.

Because of the intense interest of the press in her flight—two wire-service reporters were aboard ship—commercial communications received and transmitted on the *Itasca* were numerous. At 2:45 A.M. Howland time, radio operator Leo G. Bellarts and the reporters listening near him recognized Amelia's voice and heard her first faint message when she was fourteen hours and fifteen minutes into the flight. An hour later they heard her report the weather was "overcast," and that she was listening on 3105 kilocycles. Fifteen minutes later, at his regular reporting time, Bellarts requested that she give her position and estimated time of arrival at Howland and asked her to acknowledge their communication during her next scheduled broadcast. He received no response. At 4:53 A.M., while Bellarts was sending a voice message of the weather on 3105 kilocycles, Amelia broke in, her signal so faint and static-laden that all he could hear were the words "partly cloudy."

At 6:14 A.M., Howland time, Amelia's signal came in louder; she was about two hundred miles away. "Want bearing on 3105 kilocycles on hour. Will whistle in microphone," she said, but static prevented the radiomen from hearing her long enough to take a bearing on her. Fred Noonan had estimated the Electra would arrive at Howland at 6:30 A.M., and fifteen minutes after that, the *Itasca* heard her signal again, this time even stronger than the previous relay. She said they were about one hundred miles from the island, but this time her transmission was too brief for the radio operators to fix her position. At 7:18 A.M., transmitting on 3105 kilocycles, Bellarts, concerned that she could not hear his communications, asked her to change to 500 kilocycles so they could get a bearing on her, but received no response. At 7:42 A.M., Amelia's voice came over the radio again, with the strongest signal thus far. "We must be on you but cannot see you but gas is running low. Been unable reach you by radio. We are flying at altitude one thousand feet," she said. A second log kept on board ship and verified by witnesses recorded she mentioned having only a half hour's supply of fuel left. The *Itasca* transmitted on both 500 and 3105 kilocycles in hopes that she would hear the relays but to no avail. Her next broadcast, at 8:00 A.M., again sounded strong. "We are circling but cannot hear you. Go ahead on 7500 either now or on the schedule time of half hour." On its hourly broadcast, the *Itasca* sent its messages, and heard again from Amelia, who finally acknowledged their communication but again spoke too briefly for crewmen to take a bearing. "Please take bearing on us and answer on 3105 with voice," she asked and followed by broadcasting a five-second series of Morse dashes. Her signal was so strong that Bellarts left his position to stand on deck to listen for her engines and scan the sky for the Electra, but he didn't hear or see the airplane. The ship, meantime, could not comply with her 3105 request because the Navy's direction finder, taken ashore on Howland Island earlier to help track the Electra and powered by the *Itasca*'s gun batteries, worked only on 500 kilocycles, and the batteries were running down.

For the next forty minutes, the *Itasca* broadcast on all possible frequencies anticipating that better communications could be established with the Electra to estimate her position. At 8:44 A.M., Amelia, who had been flying for more than twenty hours, broadcast another strong signal, reaching the *Itasca* for the last time. Her strained voice and rapid speech indicated the urgency she felt as she said, "We are on the line of position 157–337. Will repeat this message on 6210 kilocycles. Wait, listening on 6210 kilocycles. We are running north and south."

In the United States, George Putnam waited for word of his wife in the Coast Guard offices in San Francisco. When he received the message sent from the *Itasca* that the ship had lost contact with her and feared she was down, he first thought that it was a mistake like the erroneous 1932 report of her Paris crash and the more recent spurious report that the Electra had been destroyed by fire when she ground-looped in Hawaii. When he realized the *Itasca* news was authentic, he took an active role in trying to locate her, scanning the news reports for any rumors that might contain a lead into Amelia's whereabouts, and asking for transmissions to be made hourly on 3105 kilocycles to her. He told reporters for the *New York Sunday Mirror*, "She has more courage than anyone I know. I am worried, of course, but I have confidence in her ability to handle any situation."

Itasca Commander Thompson waited for an hour and fifteen minutes after Amelia's last transmission, and when no further contact was made, he instituted search procedures. The visibility was good except for a bank of cumulus clouds, probably thirty or forty miles to the north and west of Howland Island. The ship had been producing heavy black smoke since dawn, and while he estimated the plume could be seen from the air for twenty miles, he reasoned that a pilot might have missed locating both the island and the ship in the glare of the bright morning sunlight.

The Electra's fuel tanks, emptied of their load, might provide the plane some buoyancy as would the fifty-five-foot wing, Thompson thought. However, the *Itasca* had no record of Amelia's course, her speed, and only the line of position, lacking any reference point that she'd given during her last transmission, so he formulated his best estimate based on fragmentary information. Baker Island, another dot on the ocean, similar in size to Howland and thirty-eight miles south, was investigated as well. Thompson requested assistance from a Navy seaplane and from the two British vessels in the area, the SS *Moorsby* and HMS *Achilles,* and soon after that, the American battleship USS *Colorado,* stationed in Hawaii, was instructed to enter the search. The PBY seaplane departed from Honolulu, maintained excellent two-way radio communications with the *Itasca* throughout its journey, but was forced to return to Pearl Harbor because of bad weather seven hundred miles north of Howland. The crew of the plane reported, "Snow, sleet, rain, electrical storms" between altitudes of two thousand and twelve thousand feet, with clouds topping eighteen thousand feet.

On the second day of the search, Mary Bea Martinelli Noonan, Fred Noonan's bride of just a few months, arrived at the San Francisco Coast Guard headquarters to await news with Putnam. Although she soon collapsed from the strain, he continued his frantic vigil for days, desperately seeking any information that could aid investigators in their task of trying to find Amelia, even consulting Amelia's friend and fellow pilot Jackie Cochran for any psychic clues she might have gathered. She believed Amelia and Noonan were alive and gave a location and the ship's name, *Itasca*, although she claimed not to have heard of the well-publicized Coast Guard cutter's name before. Searchers complied with his request to explore the areas she mentioned but with no success, and Putnam also asked them to deviate from their original pattern to comb the Phoenix Islands southeast of Howland, where she might have made a landing. This effort revealed no clues.

The airplane tender USS *Swan* explored the Gilbert Islands west of Howland, and Japanese ships stationed in the area of their country's possession, the Marshall Islands, about six hundred miles north of Howland, were asked to look in that region for the two fliers. The aircraft carrier USS *Lexington* had to travel eleven days from Santa Barbara, California, before it could lend assistance, and three destroyers, the *Drayton, Lamson,* and *Cushing,* escorted the ship to its destination and joined the mission. After arriving at Howland, the *Lexington*'s sixty-two airplanes flew three sorties each day in groups of four, scanning the restless waves for any sign of the Electra or her lost crew. Four thousand men participated in the painstaking search that eventually covered 262,281 square miles of the ocean.

Because Amelia was so well known and beloved worldwide, numerous radio operators sent signals hoping to reach her and to aid in her rescue. In addition, the *Itasca* continued to transmit, and some confusion resulted, with reports of radio signals and voice transmissions from as far away as Wyoming and as near to the area as Australia, creating flurries of excitement until they were traced back to their sources. Amateur radio operators reported hearing faint relays in Morse code, which they thought Amelia might have been able to send by holding her microphone button. Instead, they probably heard the *Itasca* trying to reestablish contact with her. The San Francisco office of the Coast Guard heard nothing from the Electra nor did the ships scattered throughout the Pacific. One particularly distressing incident occurred when an airport operator, listening to his radio, heard a simulated conversation between Amelia and the *Itasca* on the regular radio program, *The March of Time*. He reported this as his having heard Amelia, and after a chaotic rush to follow this possible lead, investigators again found only disappointment.

Another message, received at the Wailupe station in Hawaii, said, "281 North Howland Call KHAQQ Beyond North Don't Hold With Us Much Longer Above Water Shut Off." The call letters were Amelia's, and the possibility that she had been floating in the area described and was only now turning off her radio generated yet another round of optimism that came to naught. The message was later proven to be a hoax, one of countless frauds that disrupted searchers. On July 5, 1937, the *Itasca* reported seeing flares in the darkness and, thinking it might be Amelia or Noonan, sent a transmission asking the Electra to shoot another flare, which caused some newspapers in the United States to print erroneous banner headlines that she had been found. Instead, the bright light had been caused by meteors in the area. Paul Mantz, following the search from Los Angeles, told reporters Amelia had left the flares behind in the Burbank hangar and said she and Noonan had "one chance in a thousand" of survival. He thought Amelia, likely suffering from pilot fatigue, might have run out of fuel and tried to land too high over the water. The resulting plane crash, he said, would have killed both her and Noonan instantly. He suggested she might also have tried to land in rough water where "it would be quite hard to judge the distance properly, thus causing her to fly into a heavy roller, having a similar result."

The likelihood that Amelia and Noonan had not

survived became clearer with every passing hour, yet her admirers throughout the world continued to hope that she had managed to land the Electra somewhere and would return. On July 7, 1937, First Lady Eleanor Roosevelt wrote in her column, "My Day," in the *New York Telegram*, "I feel sure that if she comes through safely she will feel that what she has learned makes it all worth while. But her friends will wish science could be served without so much risk to a fine person whom many people love as a person and not as a pilot or adventurer."

More than a quarter of a million square miles of the Pacific were investigated during the immense search authorized by President Roosevelt and thought to have cost more than four million dollars. The official mission was abandoned on July 18, 1937, sixteen days after Amelia's final broadcast, but Putnam refused to give up on her. He sought the assistance of the National Geographic Society to begin a more intensive search of the Gilbert Islands, and wrote to his mother-in-law, Amy Earhart, to promise her that he would continue his efforts to find Amelia. He even asked the further assistance of the British naval vessels at his own expense. To help finance these procedures, he completed the book his wife had been writing about her world flight, giving it the title, *Last Flight*.

In 1928 before she flew across the Atlantic aboard the *Friendship*, Amelia had written a note to each of her parents and had given them to Putnam for safekeeping, to be opened only if she were lost at sea. She had assured both her mother and father that even if she failed, her adventure had been worthwhile. Before she had embarked on her world journey, she had written one of her customary preflight notes to G.P. to be opened if she did not return, and he included it in her final book. She wrote, "Please know I am aware of the hazards. I want to do it because I want to do it. Women must try to do things as men have tried. When they fail, their failure must be but a challenge to others."

Throughout the months following Amelia's disappearance Putnam and Amy Earhart grasped at any possible lead as to her fate. Countless suggestions and ideas arose, some logical but most odd, many of them coming from psychics, and several later discovered to be cruel hoaxes.

Putnam eventually took legal action to become the trustee of Amelia's estate to help pay the mounting bills, more expensive than he could afford since he had gambled everything on the world flight. He continued to send money to Amy as her daughter had done and as Amelia had requested in her will, but Amy, still distrustful of him, thought G.P. was bilking her somehow and that his motives were based on greed. He later took action to have his wife declared dead, consulting with attorneys, who successfully argued the case involved special circumstances that would allow waiver of the usual seven-year waiting period. On January 5, 1939, Amelia Earhart was officially listed as deceased.

AMELIA EARHART'S RECORDS

1928 June 17, first woman to fly across the
Atlantic Ocean in the *Friendship*.

1929 August 18–26, participant in first
Women's Air Derby; A.E. placed third.

1930 Elected first president of Ninety-Nines,
Inc.

1930 June 25–July 5, flying Lockheed Vega,
sets women's world speed record 100
kilometers (174.897).
Women's world speed record with
500-kilogram load, 171.438 mph.
Women's world speed record, 181.18 mph.

1931 Elected first woman vice president of
the National Aeronautics Association.

1931 April 8, establishes women's altitude
record in Pitcairn Autogiro, 18,415 feet.

1931 First pilot to fly Pitcairn Autogiro on
round-trip across the United States.

1932 May 20, first woman to solo the Atlantic
Ocean, piloting single-engine Lockheed
Vega. Harbor Grace, Newfoundland, to
Culmore, Ireland, fourteen hours, fifty-six
minutes.

1932 July 12–13, First woman to fly solo across the transcontinental United States, Los Angeles to Newark, nineteen hours, fourteen minutes, ten seconds.

1933 With Ruth Nichols, the first women to compete in the Bendix Race.

1935 First pilot to fly solo west to east from Honolulu to Oakland.

1935 Flies from Burbank to Mexico City, speed record of thirteen hours, thirty-two minutes.

1935 August 25, first woman to fly nonstop coast to coast across the United States, setting new cross-country distance record.

1937 June 1, takes off in attempt to fly the world at the equator. First person to fly nonstop across Red Sea to India during this attempt. Achieves twenty-two thousand miles before being lost en route from Lae, New Guinea, to Howland Island.

Theories

After the courts recognized Amelia's death in 1939, George Putnam married Jean Marie Cosigny, but continued to try to find clues to his previous wife's disappearance. Jean remembered feeling as if Amelia would just walk back into their lives one day because her presence endured and public sentiment remained optimistic that she had somehow survived. Because Amelia had been secretive about her flight, Amy Earhart thought a persistent and prevailing rumor, that her daughter might have been on a covert spy mission for the United States, to be credible. Many thought Amelia and Fred Noonan had been sent by the government to fly over Japanese holdings in the Pacific to discover whether Japan had been illegally fortifying their islands in preparation for war. If that were the case, the theory went, the two Americans likely had landed on an island in the area after they had difficulty locating Howland, and might have been captured by the Japanese.

In 1937 the Japanese had possession of the Marshall, Mariana, and Caroline Islands through a mandate instituted following World War I, and had been requested to search for Amelia, Fred Noonan, and the Electra in the Marshalls. Japan had withdrawn from the League of Nations in 1935, and although authorized by international law to do so, the organization could not wield control over the Mandated Islands under the circumstances. Because Japan had earlier invaded Manchuria and in 1936 and 1937 had made efforts to control Asia and the West Pacific, tensions ran high in the region. The United States supported an isolationist policy at the time, and Americans were not allowed to search the Japanese-held islands after the Electra was lost, although two Japanese ships in the area, the *Kamoi* and the *Koshu,* participated in the United States naval explorations in 1937. Both governments concluded the fliers had crashed into the ocean. Just days after Amelia and Noonan disappeared, Japan attacked China.

When the United States entered World War II, Putnam served as a major in the Army Air Corps, working as an intelligence officer for a B-29 squadron stationed in the China-Burmese theater, and he sought any information he could find about what might have happened to Amelia on her final flight. He even traveled throughout Saipan, where a white woman pilot had supposedly been seen before the war, but his efforts yielded nothing. Friends remarked that G.P. was a much-changed man following his famous wife's disappearance, and that he never really got over her presumed death.

Movies of the time spurred on the spy theory, with *Stand By to Die,* although fictional, using some of Amelia's adventures, and another made during the period, *Flight to Freedom,* starring Rosalind Russell and Fred MacMurray, portraying two American fliers in thinly disguised roles resembling Amelia and Noonan. The plot centered on the woman pilot's flight across the ocean to a remote island where she was to pretend to be lost so that the military could institute a search and at the same time collect intelligence about the Japanese holdings. The movie depicted the woman pilot and her navigator having an affair, and Putnam, irritated by that reflection on Amelia, filed a lawsuit, which was eventually dropped and thought to have been simply a publicity stunt for the movie.

The widespread belief that Amelia was on a reconnaissance mission when she disappeared prompted Eleanor Roosevelt to write to Muriel Morrissey to assure her that President Roosevelt would not have sent her sister on such a hazardous operation. But the rumors persisted. Some people even thought Amelia was the mysterious voice of "Tokyo Rose" during World War II, but Putnam put a stop to this ridiculous idea.

Following his military service, G.P. and his fourth wife, Margaret Haviland, purchased the Stove Pipe

Wells Inn in Death Valley, California. He died on January 4, 1950.

Amelia's mother, Amy Otis Earhart, died on October 29, 1962, at the age of ninety-three, having lived at Amelia and George's house in Toluca Lake, California, for a number of years before moving to West Medford, Massachusetts, to stay with the Morrisseys. Muriel Morrissey, who believed Amelia's plane went down in the Pacific somewhere near Howland Island, continued to spread Amelia's message by attending memorial events and writing two books about her famous sibling before her death in 1998.

In the 1960s, CBS newsman Fred Goerner studied the Amelia Earhart puzzle, after learning from a newspaper article that Josephine Blanco Akiyama, a woman who had once lived on the island of Saipan, recalled seeing a twin-engine plane flying over in 1937, and that two American fliers, a man and a woman, had been captured and killed by the Japanese. He made four trips to Saipan between 1960 and 1966, talking to numerous people there to try to solve the mystery.

He met with some frustrating resistance from the United States Navy because of its reluctance to release any information about either Amelia's disappearance or the American trust territories. He nonetheless continued his investigation. During his explorations of Tanapag Harbor he found a generator from an old two-motored aircraft with a Bendix serial number and was later guided by a former Army postal unit sergeant, Thomas Devine, to a double grave on the island thought to have been that of Amelia and Noonan. Paul Mantz (who died in a 1965 airplane crash) examined the generator and declared it to be similar to one he had installed in Amelia's Electra, but the Bendix company pursued the matter further and deemed the old part to have been a copy, possibly made by a Japanese manufacturer. Because Amelia's plane had been repaired several times along her world route, the possibility existed that the generator might have been used as a replacement part, but that could not be proven.

The bones in the grave were exhumed and examined by an anthropologist in the United States, who reported them to have been non-Caucasian and likely the remains of four people rather than two. Goerner weighed testimony of his many witnesses, one of whom recalled seeing the Electra deliberately destroyed in a fire, and another who remembered a woman being held as a prisoner until she died of dysentery, at which point the man who had been with her had been executed. Goerner speculated that Amelia and Noonan left Lae, New Guinea, and flew to Truk, one of the Caroline Islands, to observe Japanese activity there, especially noting the number of airfields. They had flown off course en route to Howland because Noonan could not get an accurate star reading in the overcast conditions they passed through on July 2, 1937, and Amelia could not reveal their position during her radio communications with the *Itasca* in order to keep their mission secret. Goerner theorized that the two ran out of fuel and crashlanded on Mili Atoll in the southeastern Marshall Islands and that Amelia was unhurt and helped Noonan, who had struck his head during the impact. On July 13, 1937, according to Goerner, the two were taken ashore by a Japanese fishing boat, then eventually to Saipan, the Japanese military headquarters in the Pacific, where they were questioned and later executed.

The Japanese capture hypothesis has largely been discounted in the intervening years while serious study of the more likely circumstances continue.

Former naval airman and Earhart author Elgen Long, who flew missions in the Howland Island region, believes Amelia encountered stronger head winds and stormier conditions than she had expected, causing the Electra to consume more fuel than planned. In addition, her charts of the region may have been incorrect, with the error showing Howland Island six miles off its actual location. The added complication of her inexperience with the radio equipment, and the communication difficulties that ensued when she tried to contact the *Itasca*, thwarted her attempts to site the ship before her engines quit and she crashed into the ocean, possibly within thirty miles of her destination. Elgen Long based his theory on discussions with *Itasca* radio operator Leo Bellarts, detailed records kept by Eric Chaters, the manager of New Guinea Airways, which were lost after 1937 but rediscovered in 1991 in Vancouver, British Columbia, and upon his own knowledge of aviation. Long reasons that after twenty hours of flight, her fuel load was too low to reach any of the surrounding islands, and that her final message to the *Itasca* was incomplete because the engine quit. She and Noonan either died in the crash or drowned.

He said, "The mystery continues until the airplane is found, and we will find it."

A deep-sea diving company, Nauticos, of Cape Porpoise, Maine, which has worked for the United States Navy, has conducted underwater explorations of the Pacific Ocean in the Howland Island region as recently as 2002 to try to discover the wreckage of the Electra. Company president David Jourdan believes the aircraft is submerged at a depth between eighteen thousand and twenty thousand feet, and while it may be in several pieces, they are likely well preserved due to the cold temperatures at that depth. Amelia's radio transmissions are also being re-created, using pattern tests, vintage radios, and scale models to help locate the plane.

During the 2002 expedition, the crew sailed on the research vessel *Davidson* and used sophisticated sonar equipment to examine the ocean for any sign of the Electra. Technical problems with the winch required the expedition to be postponed before any compelling evidence was discovered. Another expedition is planned for early 2005, and Jourdan remains confident that Nauticos will be able to pinpoint the wrecked plane.

The International Group for Historic Aircraft Recovery (TIGHAR), a nonprofit organization located in Delaware, offers another contemporary hope of completing the Earhart puzzle. Executive Director Ric Gillespie has visited the island of Nikumaroro in the Phoenix Island group seven times since 1989. He is certain he will discover definitive evidence showing Amelia crashed there and that she and Noonan lived for a time on the island as castaways.

According to the TIGHAR theory, Amelia landed on Nikumaroro (formerly Gardner Island), located about four hundred miles south of Howland on the navigational line she reported in her final radio transmission to the *Itasca*. The United States Navy conducted an aerial search of that then-uninhabited island in 1937, Gillespie said, since it was the most logical place to look and the Electra should have had enough fuel to be landed on the reef that surrounds the atoll. He believes the plane likely washed over the edge of the reef and was obscured from view during the aerial search by the surf.

"A strong island tradition" passed on by former residents of the island, inhabited during the years 1938 through 1963 and now deserted, indicates that an airplane wreck was located just off the reef when the first settlers arrived. In 1940 British colonial officer Gerald Gallagher, stationed on the island, discovered a partial skeleton and sent the bones to Fiji for analysis. The colonial physician who examined them concluded they were those of a short, stocky man. After that, the matter was dropped, and the bones disappeared. TIGHAR researchers, who have tried in vain to find the bones, studied the measurements taken by the earlier doctor and reached a different conclusion. Contemporary forensic anthropologist Dr. Karen Burns examined the measurements and found that the available data suggest the bones were most likely those of a white woman of Northern European descent, between five feet six inches and six feet tall, roughly similar in size to Amelia.

Along with the bones, Gallagher also found fragments of the sole of a woman's shoe, part of a man's shoe, and a sextant box. Researchers believe these shoe parts belonged to Amelia and Noonan. Bits of aluminum and of Plexiglas identical to that used in the manufacture of Lockheed Electras of the same model as Amelia flew have also been found, but the aluminum pieces and Plexiglas were cut into squares and used by islanders in fishing lures and were thus difficult to trace. The most recent TIGHAR trip yielded items that may have been "interior furnishings" of a twin-engine cabin-class plane like the Electra, but this has not yet been proven.

"We still have to find something that qualifies as a 'smoking gun,'" Gillespie said, "like a serial number, a part of the Electra that would be unique to that aircraft, or human remains that could be matched with D.N.A."

Currently, the organization is conducting a comprehensive study of the 184 distress calls placed after Amelia's disappearance, using signal-to-noise ratios and other criteria. Patterns indicate that some of the messages don't fit the criteria for hoaxes or misunderstood broadcasts. If one of those transmissions can be authenticated as one she sent, Gillespie says it will prove Amelia did not crash into the ocean because her radio would not have worked if the plane was afloat on the ocean.

He hopes to return to Nikumaroro in the summer of 2005 to search the area around the island with a manned submersible vehicle, to determine if the surf carried the plane off the land and into the water.

Epilogue

Amelia Earhart's heroic legacy lies within the daring spirit that survives her. Elementary schools across America, mountains, streets, and varieties of flowers bear her name, still symbolic of her "can-do" attitude. Zonta International, of which she was a member, sponsors a scholarship program for women interested in aviation, as does the Ninety-Nines. The Atchison home of her childhood is now a museum, and the Kansas town hosts an annual summer celebration in honor of her July 24 birthdate. The International Forest of Friendship, which contains trees from all fifty states and commemorates pioneers in aviation and aerospace, is located there to honor her.

In 1966 the Smithsonian Institution acquired from the Franklin Institute and placed on display the red Lockheed Vega she flew across the Atlantic.

In the intervening years since Amelia's disappearance, three women pilots have paid tribute to her memory by re-creating some of her flights. Each felt some affinity with the lost flier, not only in her own passion for aviation, but through sharing in her spirit of adventure and determination to succeed.

In 1967 Ann Pellegreno of Michigan embarked on the "Earhart Commemorative Flight," piloting a restored Lockheed Electra 10A, a plane similar to that which Amelia flew, around the world. As a relatively new pilot with just one hundred hours of airtime, she felt inspired by Amelia's final note to George Putnam, which challenged women to view failures of others as stepping-stones.

Pellegreno, accompanied by copilot William Payne of the United States Air Force, and a navigator, Bill Polhemus, did not follow Amelia's flight plan exactly but encountered similar difficulties in finding Howland Island.

Pellegreno's crew used the same navigational method Noonan used. When they came within sixty miles of Howland, they descended to one thousand feet and encountered rain squalls that obscured their view of the ocean, weather that was "uncannily similar" to that confronted by Amelia thirty years before. Even with the assistance of the modern navigational aids they brought along, and after taking a bearing on the U.S. Coast Guard cutter *Blackhaw* stationed at Howland, they had trouble locating the island.

Pellegreno and her crew successfully completed their world flight, and in 1968 their Lockheed 10A was sold to Air Canada and flown to Ottawa, placed on permanent exhibit at the Ottawa International Airport.

In 1997 Texas pilot and nursing home administrator Linda Finch, who also flies and restores vintage aircraft, re-created Amelia's world flight, honoring her 1937 trip as well as the centennial of her birth. Finch flew a Lockheed Electra 10E, refurbishing and rebuilding the plane from plans the Lockheed company used for manufacturing Amelia's, even carrying a bamboo pole that made communication possible between navigator and pilot. She flew with navigator Denny Ghirendelli and incorporated educational programs with her trip through interactive Internet hookups so that students worldwide could participate in the event. The aircraft was later flown across the Atlantic, commemorating Amelia's transatlantic flight, and displayed at the Paris Air Show.

In 2001 California periodontist Carlene Mendieta re-created another of Amelia's flights, sharing Finch's determination to help the public focus on more of Amelia's accomplishments than just the ill-fated world trip. Mendieta, a vintage aircraft owner herself with a special affinity for taildraggers, flew a privately owned, restored Avro Avian biplane across the United States to commemorate Amelia's 1928 transcontinental journey.

She began her trip on September 4, 2001, and followed Amelia's fifty-five-hundred-mile route closely, flying at a speed of about ninety miles per hour, and sometimes descending to altitudes of five hundred feet to view the landscape. Following the September 11 terror attacks in New York City and Washington, D.C., Mendieta was grounded for several days in Hobbs, New Mexico, due to the restrictions placed on flight in the United States but she refused to cancel her trip. The plane, owned by vintage aircraft aficionado and entrepreneur Greg Herrick, was, like Amelia's, an open cockpit craft with no radio, and Mendieta navigated with a road map and a compass as Amelia had done.

Three weeks of almost constant flight for Mendieta only increased her respect for Amelia who she said was "a heck of a pilot and even a better navigator" to have made the trip.

Amelia's achievements far outshine the tragedy of the single incomplete flight that ended her life. Although George Putnam's keen promotional efforts ensured her fame and status as a celebrity flier, Amelia captivated the public with her engaging modesty, her ability to laugh at herself, and her winning attitude. During a time when it was considered unfashionable for women to seek careers, she demonstrated through her own example that opportunities thought to have been reserved for men were available to women as well. In marrying George Putnam, she again pushed the limits of the social mores of the times, expecting her husband to allow her the freedom to pursue her dreams. She proved, too, that women could combine marriage with their careers, successfully uniting her airborne ventures with her husband's business prowess. She shared her experiences with women students at Purdue University, encouraging them to pursue studies in the fields they chose rather than relying upon tradition or the preferences of their families.

As a young pilot, she was "full of missionary zeal for the cause of aviation," and sometimes wore a dress or a suit when she flew rather than donning shirt and trousers, hoping to convince the public that flying was as routine as sitting in one's home and to encourage them to share in the delight she found aloft. Later, she flew aboard commercial airliners, beckoning people to ride along and enjoy the speed and romance of flight while spurring their interest in the fledgling commercial aviation industry.

In one of the newsreels filmed before her final flight, her blue-gray eyes sparkled with the anticipation of the forthcoming trip as she confidently answered the questions of reporters.

Although her skills as a pilot had been questioned by some throughout her career, she persevered, seeking the advice and assistance of expert fliers when necessary. Her accomplishments during the world flight tested her hard-won skills. On that journey, despite a crash on takeoff in Hawaii, she soldiered on, eventually logging nearly one thousand miles each day during an intense three-week period, performing often precarious takeoffs and landings, and flying over diverse and often hostile terrain through a variety of adverse weather conditions.

Her previous long-distance flights—across the Atlantic and Pacific Oceans, the Gulf of Mexico, and the United States—in hindsight served as practice for her longest attempted trip following the equator, but Amelia flew simply because she loved to fly. The logs of the *Friendship* and later flights are filled with her eloquent descriptions of clouds and landscapes below. She enjoyed the allure of flight from the first time she rode in an airplane, and in the air she escaped her earthly concerns and responsibilities for just a little while.

Following her transpacific flight she wrote "the lure of flying is the lure of beauty," stating that "the reason flyers fly, whether they know it or not, is the esthetic appeal of flying."

For Amelia Earhart, the sky was no limit.

ACKNOWLEDGMENTS AND SOURCES

Quotations of Amelia Earhart are included here through the permission extended by her niece, Amy Kleppner, as represented by CMG Worldwide, Inc., whose Web site is *www.CMGWorldwide.com*. I consulted Amelia's own books, *20 Hrs., 40 Mins.: Our Flight in the Friendship* (G. P. Putnam's Sons, 1928), *The Fun of It* (Press of Braunworth & Co., Inc., 1932), and *Last Flight* (Crown Trade Paperbacks, 1988), and her numerous articles for *Cosmopolitan* and other periodicals.

George Palmer Putnam's *Soaring Wings* (Harcourt, Brace, 1939), a biography of Amelia, and *Wide Margins* (Harcourt, Brace, 1942), an autobiography, were both especially helpful here with personal details, as were the books of her sister, Muriel Morrissey: *Courage Is the Price* (McCormick-Armstrong Publishing, 1963) and

Amelia, My Courageous Sister (Osborne Publisher, 1987), written with Carol L. Osborne.

Also of great value in my research were Doris Rich's *Amelia Earhart: A Biography* (Smithsonian Institution Press, 1989) and Mary S. Lovell's *The Sound of Wings* (St. Martin's Press, 1989). Others consulted were John Burke's *Winged Legend* (Ballantine, 1970), Paul Briand's *Daughter of the Sky* (Pyramid, 1967), and Jean L. Backus's *Letters from Amelia* (Beacon Press, 1982).

The Schlesinger Library at Radcliffe College in Cambridge, Massachusetts, and Purdue University in West Lafayette, Indiana, and the Library of Congress house large Earhart collections. Additional Earhart memorabilia can be found at the Amelia Earhart Birthplace Museum in Atchison, Kansas, and the headquarters of The Ninety-Nines, Inc., Oklahoma City, Oklahoma.

My thanks to Patty Williams at the National Air and Space Museum of the Smithsonian, and librarians Val Vasquez, Mary Ann Harlow, Jennifer Mayer, and Larry Schmidt at the University of Wyoming in Laramie, Wyoming.

For information on the theories surrounding her disappearance, I am indebted to Fred Goerner's *The Search for Amelia Earhart* (Dell, 1966), *Amelia Earhart's Shoes* by Thomas King, Randall Jacobson, Karen Burns, and Kenton Spading (AltaMira Press, 2001), and several television documentaries, notably National Geographic's "On Assignment," The Travel Channel's *In Search of Amelia Earhart* (Pioneer Productions, 2002), and the

PBS documentary *The Final Hours: Amelia Earhart's Last Flight* (Romeo Delta Productions, 2001). I consulted also the records for the U.S. Coast Guard cutter *Itasca,* the report of the U.S. Navy's search, and records relating to the 1937 search for Amelia held in the National Archives. I learned more through a telephone interview with Nauticos president David Jourdan and on the Nauticos Web site, *www.nauticos.com.* Ric Gillespie of TIGHAR (*www.tighar.org*), and moderator of the Internet Earhart Forum, also gave a telephone interview. The official Earhart Web site, *www.ameliaearhart.com,* contains some background information, helpful links, and updates on searches and theories. For background on various makes of airplanes and their specifications, I consulted *www.aerofiles.com.*

Information on Amelia's flight re-creations are found in Ann Pellegreno's *World Flight* (Iowa State University Press, 1971), Linda Finch's *No Limits* (World Flight, 1996), and the PBS and Travel Channel documentaries mentioned above as well as the Web site *www.amelia flight.com* detailing the biplane flight of Dr. Carlene Mendieta.

I am especially grateful for the expertise of retired corporate pilot Harvey Pardun and the assistance of Jim Dunrud. Special thanks to my husband, Eugene W. Walck, Jr., and Cid, Marilyn, and Eugene Walck, Sr. Friends Beverley Edens, Marilyn Rummel, Candy Moulton, Jim Crutchfield, Bill Groneman, W. C. Jameson, Laurie Wagner Buyer, Rod Miller, Elaine Long,

Nancy Curtis, and Kris Wendtland also helped. For the assistance, encouragement, and friendship of general editor Dale L. Walker, I am forever grateful; also special thanks to literary agent Nat Sobel, originator of this series, and to Tom Doherty, publisher.

OTHER SOURCES

Balchen, Bernt. *Come North with Me*. New York: E. P. Dutton, 1958.

Boyne, Walter J. *The Smithsonian Book of Flight*. New York: Wings Books, 1987.

Chapman, Sally Putnam. *Whistled Like a Bird*. New York: Warner Books, 1997.

Cochran, Jacqueline. *The Stars at Noon*. Boston and Toronto: Little, Brown, 1954.

Corn, Joseph. *Winged Gospel*. Baltimore and London: Johns Hopkins University Press, 2001.

Dwiggins, Don. *Hollywood Pilot*. New York: Doubleday, 1967.

————. *They Flew the Bendix Race*. Philadelphia and New York: J. B. Lippincott, 1965.

Gunston, Bill. *The Illustrated History of Propeller Airliners*. New York: Exeter, n.d.

History of the Ninety-Nines. Oklahoma City: The Ninety-Nines, International Organization of Women Pilots, 1979.

Jenkinson, Sir Anthony. *America Came My Way*. London: Arthur Barker, 1936.

Lindbergh, Anne Morrow. *Hour of Gold, Hour of Lead*. New York: Harcourt Brace Jovanovich, 1973.

Lindbergh, Charles. *We*. New York: Grosset & Dunlap, 1927.

Mosley, Leonard. *Lindbergh: A Biography*. New York: Doubleday and Company, 1976.

Nevin, David. *The Pathfinders*. Chicago: Time-Life Books, 1980.

Nichols, Ruth. *Wings for Life*. Philadelphia and New York: J. P. Lippincott, 1957.

Planck, Charles E. *Women with Wings*. New York: Harper Brothers, 1942.

Railey, Captain Hilton H. *Touch'd by Madness*. New York: Carrick & Evans, 1938.

Smith, Elinor. *Aviatrix*. New York and London: Harcourt Brace Jovanovich, 1981.

Smith, Henry Ladd. *Airways: History of Commercial Flight in the United States*. New York: Alfred A. Knopf, 1942.

Streeter, Dan. *An Arctic Rodeo*. G. P. Putnam's Sons, 1929.

Southern, Neta Snook. *I Taught Amelia to Fly*. New York: Vantage, 1974.

Thaden, Louise. *High, Wide, and Frightened*. New York: Stackpole Sons, 1938.

Vidal, Gore. "Love of Flying," *The New York Review of Books*. 17 January 1985.

Ware, Susan. *Still Missing*. New York: W. W. Norton, 1993.

Index

Index

Index

Lori Van Pelt is the author of *Dreamers and Schemers,* a historical Wyoming series for High Plains Press. Her short fiction appears in the national anthologies *American West* (Forge, 2001), *White Hats* (Berkley, 2002), *Black Hats* (Berkley, 2003), and *Hot Biscuits* (University of New Mexico Press, 2002). Her own collection of short fiction, *At Frontier's Edge,* is forthcoming from the University of New Mexico Press.

She lives with her husband, Eugene Walck, Jr., on his family's ranch near Saratoga, Wyoming.